2⁻

D0645361

Honey, I'm Homemade

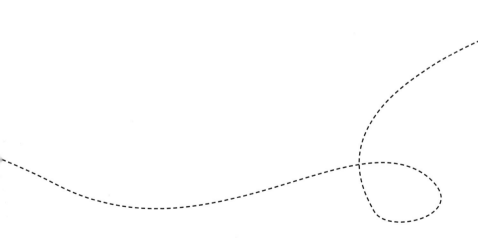

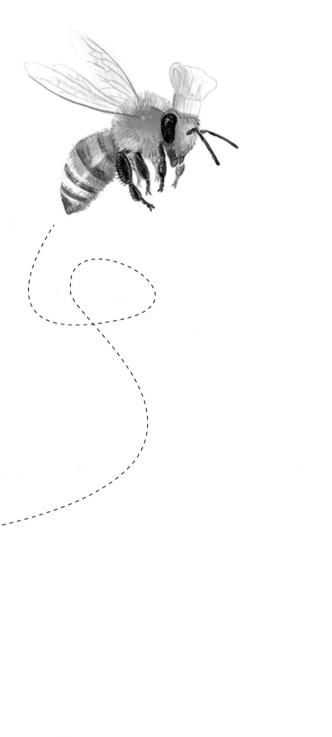

Honey, I'm Homemade

**SWEET TREATS FROM THE BEEHIVE
ACROSS THE CENTURIES
AND AROUND THE WORLD**

Edited by
MAY
BERENBAUM

Illustrated by Nils Cordes

University of Illinois Press
Urbana, Chicago, and Springfield

Library of Congress Cataloging-in-Publication Data
Berenbaum, M. (May)
Honey, I'm homemade : sweet treats
from the beehive across the centuries and
around the world / edited by May Berenbaum;
illustrated by Nils Cordes.
p. cm.
Includes bibliographical references and index.
ISBN 978-0-252-07744-9 (pbk. : alk. paper)
1. Cookery (Honey). 2. Honey. I. Title.
TX767.H7B43   2010
641.6'8—dc22   2010017097

To the memory of Hermilda Listeman

Contents

Preface

In August 2009, as I started this project, I did a quick search in the book section of Amazon.com on the phrase *honey recipes* and ended up with 1,813 hits. This outcome logically leads to the question of whether there is need for honey-recipe book number 1,814. After all, there are honey cookbooks for connoisseurs, vegetarian Jews, dieters, and refined-sugar haters. A lot of them have been written by beekeepers or assembled by beekeeping associations, groups whose ranks might be expected to be well-versed in the use of honey in all kinds of dishes. Although I'm an entomologist, I'm not in any sense of the word a beekeeper. At various intervals during my life I've been a bee landlord—other entomologists have kept bees on property I own—but I've never personally had a hive I could call my own or been involved in the production of honey. Truth be told, I'm a little afraid of honey bees—and not just because they can sting. The stings are a manageable risk. What I find unnerving about bees is how eerily talented they are and how profoundly different from the million-plus other species of insects.

So, I've come to honey bees and, consequently, honey fairly late in more than thirty-five years as an independent scientist. For years I've studied how insects eat plants and lately have become fascinated with the extraordinary capacity of the honey bee to take a plant product—nectar—and process it into a unique and unusual food. Happily, that ability has in turn conferred upon people the ability to create all kinds of unique and unusual foods. That's the thing about cooking with honey—every time honey is collected from a hive, it's the unique product of a particular set of flowers at a certain time, processed and stored by a particular group of bees. Honey is more than a snapshot of a time and place—it's the taste of a time and place.

Because of the power of honey to evoke a particular time and place, recipes with honey tend to take on personal significance. That's one reason I thought I'd undertake this project. I'm not a particularly gifted cook, but I've had the privilege of knowing a few. As befits the honey bee, a gleaner that collects nectar from an extraordinary diversity of sources, I've tapped into the collective experience of an extraordinary diversity of people. Hermilda Listeman was a prime inspiration for this project. Hermilda was my husband's cousin in Collinsville, Illinois, older than he by many years. Hermilda had an abiding interest in all things culinary, and over nine decades she collected cookbooks and recipes. She was no mere collector, though; she tested, improved, and annotated recipes for close to ninety years. Ultimately, her cookbook collection grew to exceed three thousand volumes; in 2000 she donated most of her collection to the University of Illinois at Urbana-Champaign library. But her personal notebooks, thousands of pages written painstakingly in longhand and meticulously annotated and documented, she gave to my daughter, Hannah. We didn't see Herm very often—she lived 150 miles away—but we tried to visit at least once a year. The best time to visit, from Herm's perspective, was during the Christmas holidays; even into her nineties, she delighted in presenting visitors with amazing platters heaped high with cookies she had baked with recipes from her collection. When she discovered how much Hannah enjoys baking, she must have decided that, when she could no longer bake, she would bequeath her ninety years of experience to a young enthusiast. Around 2005, at the age of ninety, Herm began assembling boxes of personal notebooks, which she shipped to Hannah.

Those recipes were the beginning of this project. Hannah graciously allowed me access to Herm's collection. Reading through just a fraction of her notes, I found at least three dozen dessert recipes featuring honey. Others turned up in the massive community cookbook collection (more than 640 volumes) she donated to the University of Illinois library; a digitization project made these much easier to search. Herm's enormous collection of material not only provided the core structure for this collection but also gave me the confidence that a collection of honey dessert recipes was an achievable goal.

The bakers in my family weren't quite as conscientious about writing down recipes as was Hermilda, but a few choice ones that include honey were preserved—among them my grandmother's legendary challah, my mother's amazing teyglach, and my Aunt Ruth's mandelbread, which I adapted and named Apiscotti to submit to (and win!) the Pollinator Partnership Don't Dessert Pollinators recipe contest.

I also recruited friends and colleagues in the entomological community and asked them to look through their family recipe collections. Because entomology is an international enterprise, the effort yielded family recipes from around the world. And because this project was designed to benefit a science outreach center developed by the University of Illinois Department of Entomology, the University of Illinois Pollinatarium, the first freestanding science center in the nation devoted to flowering plants and their pollinators, I dug through our departmental archives to find the correspondence of Vern Milum (1894–1972), the first professor of apiculture at the University of Illinois at Urbana-Champaign. Milum was a tireless advocate for bees and beekeeping, and his correspondence and publications proved rich sources of honey recipes. I also pored over a half century of annual reports of the Illinois State Beekeepers Association to find recipes that might still work. I must confess that due to time and talent constraints I did not actually try every recipe in this collection, relying instead on the collective wisdom and experience of the contributors and on the remarkable ability of even a little honey to make everything taste good. So far, though, all that have been tested have proved to be delicious.

The honey bee is all about altruism—unselfish behavior for the good of the colony. Not inappropriately, this book is also about altruism—reciprocal altruism. We're hoping that the sale of this volume will foster interest in (and sales of) honey and at the same time, as kind of a payback to the bees, help maintain the University of Illinois Pollinatarium. More than three-quarters of all flowering plant species depend on animal pollinators in order to reproduce, so pollination is a key process that sustains all kinds of ecological communities around the world. Thus, pollination sustains most of the earth's inhabitants, including species *Homo sapiens*; about one-third of the diet consumed by people around the world—the part with most of the vitamins and minerals—is the result of the pollinator-plant interaction. As the world's only truly successfully managed pollinator, the honey bee is of special importance to humans.

There's no question that honey is an important commodity; in the United States, the 2008 honey crop was valued at more than $226 million. But this value is dwarfed by the contributions of the honey bee to the U.S. economy as a managed pollinator. Every year, the honey bee's pollination services contribute close to $20 billion to American agriculture. Because so much depends on honey bees, the Pollinatarium is dedicated to increasing awareness and appreciation of all pollinators, in particular making people aware of the remarkable contributions of *Apis mellifera*—the premier pollinator partner of people around the globe.

Honey, I'm Homemade

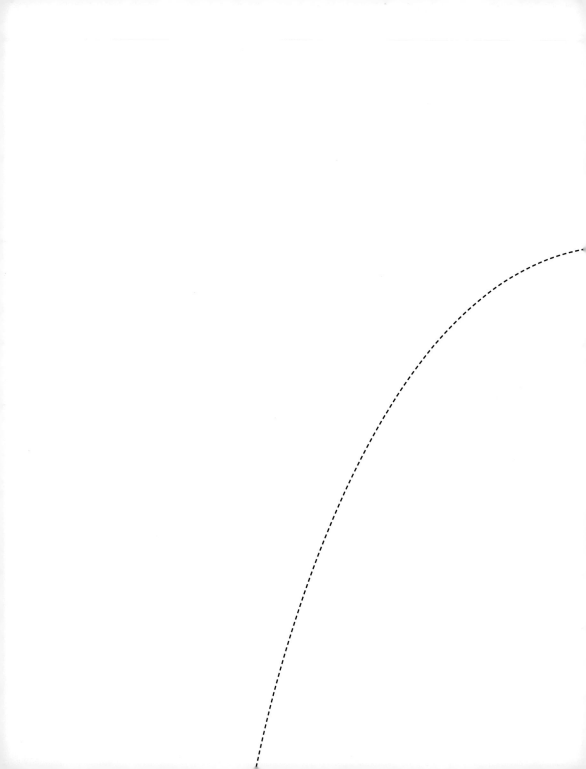

Chapter 1

Honey: The A-Bee-Cs

*H*oney is, simply put, the nectar of flowers, collected, transported, regurgitated, concentrated, biochemically processed, and packaged by *Apis mellifera,* the Western honey bee. Honey bees use sugar-rich nectar as the foundation for a supplementary food for their baby grubs and as an energy source for workers. Its inauspicious beginnings notwithstanding, honey has been a highly valued human commodity for millennia. In fact, the oldest artistic depictions of insects are cave paintings of honey bees disturbed by a human honey hunter. More than a hundred such rock art images in over a dozen countries in three continents have been found to date; those in Europe date back six thousand years, and some in Africa may be more than ten thousand years old. In every case, human figures are depicted clinging perilously to slender ropes or ladders removing honey while clouds of angry bees surround them. Around the world, people have long been aware of the remarkable nature of honey.

Honey has proved worth the effort expended to swipe it from bees—it is, after all, one of very few concentrated sources of sweetness available in nature. Biologically speaking, the human species, *Homo sapiens,* has a sweet tooth—or, more accurately, a sweet tongue. On the tip of the tongue are taste buds, or papillae, equipped with nerve cells specifically wired to respond to sweetness. The ability to taste sweet substances has been extremely useful throughout the history of humans. In nature, most potential foods that taste sweet are safe; natural poisons tend to be sour or bitter. Thus, it is not surprising that tasting sweet substances is a source of pleasure—it's a potent reward and reinforcement for finding something safe to eat.

Compared to most of the other natural sources of sweetness, honey is relatively easy to obtain. It comes conveniently packaged in little wax containers, essentially ready to eat without further preparation—unless you consider outrunning or outsmarting hordes of angry bees as part of the preparation. It is also available in most places year-round. Sugar from sugarcane, a reedy plant in the grass family native to tropical South Asia, requires harvesting the plants, crushing their stems, collecting the juice, cleaning up contaminants, and boiling down the syrup, a process that consumes precious combustible fuel. Maple syrup, made from the sap of North American maple trees, requires waiting for spring, drilling holes in many trunks, tapping trees, waiting for sap to run out, collecting the sap, and boiling it down for days at temperatures exceeding 212 degrees. Just about any other plant juice—agave nectar, date palm syrup, sorghum syrup—requires weeks of waiting, days of harvesting, and hours and hours of boiling at high temperature at the cost of using up valuable fuel.

So it's not that surprising that beehives, which can contain upwards of two hundred pounds of honey, have been tempting targets for enterprising humans. At first, honey was just stolen from bees, at considerable risk to life and limb. A few cultures in the world still make a living in this way. The Veddas in the forests of Sri Lanka, for example, are among several southeastern Asian indigenous people who rely upon bees to meet most of their material needs. Although Europeans have had to make do with only one species of *Apis,* the Veddas interact with several. *Apis dorsata* live in high trees on hillsides; *Apis indica* nest in hollow trees and rock crevices; and the dwarf bee, *Apis florea,* inhabit rock ledges. Honey is collected with the use of long ladders, bamboo canes, and smoking torches.

Most likely due to a desire to make the honey supply more reliable and less life-threatening, the semidomestication of bees—beekeeping—began very early in human history. Recent archeological excavations revealed the remains of an active honey industry dating back to 900 BCE in the ancient city of Rehov in what is now Israel. More than thirty intact hives, made of unfired clay and neatly stacked, were recovered from the ruins. Temple and tomb art dating to 2400 BCE depicts similar scenes. The sun temple of Neuserre, close to Cairo and dating to the Fifth Dynasty, depicts honey processing and packaging, and hieroglyphs that are three thousand years old show sales records. Ancient Egyptians also made mead, or honey wine, probably the world's oldest alcoholic beverage.

In ancient Greece, honey bees were kept in clay hives etched on the inside with ridges to provide a rough surface for the workers to use to anchor the comb. Honey is mentioned not only in the philosophical works of Plato and Democritus but also in Homer's epics, *The Odyssey* and *The Iliad.* The honey of Attica, a region approximately forty square miles in size, was particularly well regarded for its medicinal properties, and by the fifth century BCE more than twenty thousand hives were maintained there. Like the Egyptians, the Greeks fermented honey to produce wine and often mixed it with grape wine to produce a beverage called *oenomel;* according to *The Odyssey,* honey was also an ingredient in *kykeon,* a sort of barley gruel mixed with wine and goat cheese.

The ancient Romans were also avid beekeepers, maintaining colonies in no fewer than nine types of hives ranging from simple hollow logs to elaborate woven wicker structures. Virgil's *Georgics,* a treatise on agricultural practices of the day, includes an entire volume (Volume 4) devoted to beekeeping in verse. Athenæus's *Deipnoso-phistae,* a dialogue on controversies of the day, includes information on meals and how to prepare them; among the recipes was one for *enkhytoi,* a honey cake made from eggs, honey, and flour. Most of what is known of Roman-era cooking, however, comes from a collection of recipes known collectively as *Apicius.* References to honey abound—in *dulcia,* or honey-sweetened pastries, cakes and breads topped with honey, and honey puddings. Beyond desserts, honey was used to cure or glaze meats and sweeten beverages, including *mulsum,* a honey-sweetened wine.

Long before the Romans conquered ancient Britain, the locals practiced bee-keeping (as well as honey hunting). Honey was a staple not only for cooking but also for making mead. It was held in such high value that taxes, tolls, and tributes were often paid in honey. By the twelfth century, beekeepers in Britain were using skeps, upright hives made of coiled straw, although the concept likely originated earlier on the continent, with Germanic tribes west of the Elbe River. The word *honey* also derives from the ancient Britons (etymologically entering the language as the Old English *hunig*). Beekeeping and the use of bee products (including wax for candles) spread throughout Europe, and honey was integrated into most cuisines.

Reluctant to leave their principal sweetener behind, European colonists brought honey bees with them to the New World. Honey bees survived the Atlantic cross-ing by 1622, and escaped swarms established populations of feral bees across the continent. Although sugar supplanted honey as the principal sweetener in the United States, beekeeping did not disappear. Rather, apiculture underwent its most radical transformation in centuries in 1851, in Philadelphia, Pennsylvania. There, the Rev. Lorenzo L. Langstroth, an avid beekeeper, invented the first practical movable frame hive, designed so that a comb could be removed without destroying the rest of the hive. Langstroth's hive design, which had wooden frames around the comb that could be moved in and out of the hive box with ease, separate honey compartments, and tiered boxes that could be picked up and transported individually, is still the favored design in honey-producing countries around the world.

How Bees Make Honey

Honey may be considered by humans to be unprocessed, but in fact it is highly processed—the processor just happens to have six, instead of two, legs. Honey bees for the most part depend on flowers for food, a challenge inasmuch as flowers are not particularly abundant, predictable, or long-lived plant parts. The principal raw materials of the honey bee diet—pollen and nectar—change in availability and location over the season. Their sophisticated social structure and ability to communicate allow honey bees to survive on such unpredictable resources. They famously "dance" to convey directional information to hive mates. Foragers that find a rich nectar source return to the hive and communicate its location and distance by performing a dance. The "waggle dance," performed when the nectar source is more than three hundred feet from the hive, conveys information about distance and location. The dance is basically in the shape of a figure eight. The number of circuits completed on the comb and the number of times a dancing bee waggles her abdomen on the central part of the 8 indicate the distance; the angle of the straightaway run, relative to the vertical line of the comb, represents the angle of the nectar source relative to the sun. Because bees can see polarized light and thus can identify the sun's location even under cloudy conditions, honey bee "GPS with turn-by-turn directions" works in all kinds of weather.

The sophisticated communication system of the honey bee—the only symbolic language known in an invertebrate and rivaling human communication for precision—is incredibly handy for utilizing a resource—nectar—that is unpredictable and ephemeral. Whatever their species, individual flowers generally produce only tiny quantities of nectar, so up to one hundred thousand loads of nectar are required to produce a kilogram (2.2 pounds) of honey. One load of nectar, however, can require visiting at least a thousand individual flowers, so the 2.2 pounds of honey are the result of visits to as many as ten million flowers. Depending on how close together the flowers grow, visiting ten million may necessitate flying up to 240,000 miles—nearly the equivalent of circumnavigating the earth ten times. Bees have certainly earned their reputation for busyness.

Nectar is generally concealed in floral structures in some way (to reduce its vulnerability to visitors who take nectar without pollinating). Honey bees are equipped with highly modified mouthparts that form a tongue—a kind of lapping-sucking structure—with which to remove nectar. A forager visiting a flower swallows the nectar she collects, but it doesn't go into an ordinary stomach;—it is diverted to a sacklike honey stomach for transport back to the hive. Once a forager returns to the hive, she regurgitates the load and in that way delivers it to a hive bee, which then begins the process of converting nectar into honey. Divested of her burden, the forager is free to go out again in search of more nectar.

Nectar is mostly water with a low concentration of sugars; the first step in converting it to honey is to reduce the water content from about 80 to 90 percent to about 13 to 18 percent. Hive bees concentrate the nectar by regurgitating droplets onto their tongues over and over again—up to two hundred times. While some bees are regurgitating nectar, others are busy fanning their wings up to twenty-five thousand times per minute to circulate air and accelerate evaporation.

Evaporation is only one of the chemical changes involved in converting nectar into honey. The honey bee's saliva contains an enzyme, invertase, which converts sucrose, a complex sugar (called a disaccharide because it has two component parts) into its component simple sugars (monosaccharides), fructose and glucose. Breaking down sucrose into its component monosaccharides is essentially pre-digesting it, making it easy for grubs and workers to process. From the human perspective, the conversion also makes honey taste sweeter; fructose is about 70 percent sweeter than sucrose to humans. Also mixed with the nectar is glucose oxidase, an enzyme in honey bee saliva that reacts with glucose in nectar to produce gluconic acid and hydrogen peroxide. Hydrogen peroxide acts as a sterilizing agent in honey, and gluconic acid lowers its pH, which also discourages microbial growth.

After all of the biochemical processing is complete, the incipient honey is packaged by placing it into wax cells, where it continues to lose water until it reaches its final concentration. Honey processing does not end with reducing water content; before the honey is capped with wax it sits in the hive for a few days. As it happens, at the hive temperature of about 95 degrees, many potentially toxic nectar constituents that have been concentrated break down. One of the great advances in the history of human civilization was the discovery of fire and with it the invention of cooking, a method of food processing that helped to reduce toxicity of plant foods. Honey bees beat humans to the idea of cooking by about sixty million years.

Once processed, the honey will keep for days, weeks, months, or even years. Honey resists decay for several reasons, the principal one being that microbes cannot grow well in honey because of its low water content. Living cells require water to survive. In fact, mead, wine made from fermented honey, can be produced fairly easily by introducing a small amount of water into honey, which will allow yeasts to flourish. Honey's acidic pH also discourages microbial growth, and many nectars that are made into honey contain plant chemicals that are toxic to microbes. There are archaeological excavations at which honey in good condition has been unearthed in sealed containers that are more than a thousand years old.

Although bees are responsible for many of honey's most desirable properties, plants must get some credit, too. Honey color is a function of the pigments that are present in plant nectar. The "bouquet" of honey is a function of the essential oils produced by flowers to attract pollinators. Nectar also happens to be the source of vitamins and minerals in honey. Not inappropriately, the B-vitamins (bee-vitamins?), which are water-soluble, are present in abundance. Vitamin C, another water-soluble vitamin, can also be found in some honeys. The fat-soluble vitamins, including A, E, and K, are present in trace amounts. Nectar also is the source of minerals—potassium, abundant in nectar, is consequently abundant in honey, and calcium, magnesium, sodium, phosphorus and sulfur occur in smaller amounts.

To be fair, nectar is also occasionally the source of toxins. Some plants infuse their nectar with poisonous substances to deter inappropriate visitors, and, occasionally, bees collect this nectar and concentrate it to produce honey that can either make them sick or, sometimes, do the same to humans. Toxic honeys, however, are very rare; bees seem to do a good job of screening nectars for toxins before processing them.

One potentially toxic material that occasionally makes its way into honey comes from soil, not plants. *Clostridium botulinum* is the bacterium that causes botulism;

it can live in the soil, where it forms inert spores. Bees can pick up these spores as a consequence of foraging, and occasionally the spores make their way into honey. Ingested by an adult, they pass harmlessly through the digestive tract because they cannot germinate in the acidic conditions of the gut. The digestive tract of an infant less than a year old is significantly less acidic than that of an adult, so there is a small chance that the spores could germinate after ingestion. The active bacterium produced by the spore secretes a toxin that can induce paralysis (the same substance is found in Botox antiwrinkle injections). This is the reason that honey, and all other fresh agricultural products, should not be given to infants less than a year old.

Why Bees Eat Honey

Bees go to great lengths to make honey for a good reason: it is the most important source of food energy for both grubs and adults. Honey is remarkably energy-rich; one kilogram (2.2 pounds) provides between three thousand and 3,400 calories. By contrast, fruit-feeding insects acquire only two to four hundred calories, on average, per kilogram. Leaf-feeding insects have it even worse, acquiring only one to two hundred calories per kilogram.

Bees require a concentrated source of energy in order to maintain their energy-intensive lifestyle. The honey bee is one of very few insects that maintain a functional colony all year long, and in the winter bees must work hard to keep the hive warm. To keep themselves warm when temperatures drop, bees huddle in a tight cluster and eat honey, which provides the energy needed to shiver and generate metabolic heat. Workers take turns rotating to the outside of the cluster, where their hairy bodies insulate the cluster and cut down on heat loss. By forming these clusters, honey bees can maintain their hive temperatures at 63 degrees Fahrenheit, even if temperatures outside drop as low as eighteen degrees below zero.

Honey is more than metabolic fuel to heat the hive; it is the principal fuel for manufacturing glandular secretions. Wax, for example, is the product of glands in the abdomen of workers that are about a week old. Honey provides the metabolic energy needed for producing these glandular secretions; from eight to nine pounds are consumed to yield one pound of wax.

Animal, Vegetable, or Mineral?

Clearly, one thing honey is not is sucrose, the premier sweetener of the entire population of the world. Sucrose is a crystalline chemical compound. It is manufactured by all plants as the end product of photosynthesis, the process by which plants use light energy to convert carbon dioxide and water into chemical energy. Technically, then, it is a carbohydrate, the result of the chemical union of carbon dioxide and water. The simplest carbohydrates are made up of six carbon atoms, twelve hydrogen atoms, and six oxygen molecules. Among the most widespread of the simple six-carbon sugars are glucose and fructose. These six-carbon monosaccharides can combine to form larger carbohydrates. Sucrose, with a molecular formula of $C12H_{22}O_{11}$, is one such (slightly) larger carbohydrate—it is a disaccharide, made up of one molecule of glucose and one molecule of fructose. In pure form it is a white crystalline powder with no perceptible odor; its most distinctive attribute is sweetness.

Sucrose is known to most people as table sugar, but it was not always freely available on tables in sugar bowls. Sucrose was once such a rare commodity that it could be obtained only in apothecary shops for medicinal purposes. Although it is made by all plants, sugarcane (*Saccharum officinale*), a tropical grass species, manufactures it in huge quantities; sugar can be extracted in crystalline form by pressing the plants and extracting the sucrose-rich syrup. This practice was prohibitively expensive until Europeans, desperate for cheap sweeteners to put in their new, exotic beverages (coffee, tea, and chocolate), hit upon the idea of enslaving Africans and other nonwhite populations to perform the arduous work associated with growing, harvesting, and processing sugarcane. Once the price dropped, table sugar began to pass honey in popularity. By the nineteenth century it was so firmly entrenched in France that when sugar supplies from the Caribbean were cut off during the Napoleonic Wars the emperor promoted the cultivation of sugar beets (*Beta vulgaris*), a temperate-zone vegetable native to Europe with roots rich in sucrose, so the demand for sugar could be met through domestic sources. Today, almost one-third of the world's sucrose supply comes from sugar beets.

Sucrose replaced honey for more than economic (and chauvinistic) reasons. As a pure compound, it has a number of attributes that make it highly desirable for baking. Sucrose melts at a relatively low temperature (367 degrees Fahrenheit, often used for baking), which adds a distinctive color and flavor to pastries, cakes, and breads. Sugar can blend well with shortening such that its crystals create minute air spaces in baked goods, making them lighter and fluffier. Mixed with shortening, sugar can raise the temperature at which liquid batters solidify, allowing leavening agents such as baking soda more time to produce carbon dioxide and provide more structure to capture the carbon dioxide. More so than honey, sugar can act as a flavor-enhancer, largely because it interacts more efficiently with sugar receptors on the tongue, and thus it has become a valuable ingredient in soups and stews that otherwise might taste acidic (e.g., anything with tomatoes).

Every jar of honey is unique and distinctive whereas every bowl of refined table sugar is essentially identical to every other bowl of sugar. Its complete and utter lack of character is its virtue; it is totally reliable and reproducible. For the more adventurous eaters, however, sucrose cannot compare with honey.

Table sugar is unambiguous, a plant product with a single chemical formula, but honey is something else altogether. Sugar begins and ends with plant tissues; honey, derived from plant nectar, ultimately comes from an animal source. Discussions of how to classify honey have been ongoing since biblical times. In the Old Testament, dietary laws in the Book of Leviticus clearly spell out what is kosher and thus permissible to eat and what is *treyf* (forbidden). Insects other than locusts and their relatives are definitely not kosher; only insects that have knees above their feet qualify. So, according to Leviticus, eating bees is verboten. Honey, though, is a different story. The earliest reference to honey in the Old Testament is in the Book of Exodus, where it appears four times. Honey itself is not mentioned in the Book of Leviticus, which lays out the dietary laws and clearly stipulates that bees are not kosher. Discussions of whether "bee-honey" is kosher are relegated to the Mishna, a written compilation of oral traditions that dates back to 200 CE. In general, any product of a nonkosher animal must be considered nonkosher. An exception, however, is made for honey because "even though they bring it into their bodies, it is not a *product* of their bodies [it is stored there but not produced there]" ("Why Is Honey Kosher?"). Honey thus is literally exceptional with respect to kosher laws.

Even better—according to the Gemara, a collection of rabbinical reflections on the Mishna written around 500 CE, pure honey is automatically kosher (Bechoros

7b) and needs no rabbinical supervision or oversight by a *mashgiach* (kosher supervisor) (Vayikra 11:21). Moreover, although the dietary laws in Leviticus prohibit mixing milk and meat, honey is considered pareve—neither milk nor meat—and therefore consumable with just about any type of food.

World trade in the nineteenth century opened contentious discussion about the classification of honey. In Britain, it is classified as an animal product along with milk and eggs, as it is in India. During the 1940s, vegans, vegetarians who consume nothing of animal origin, weighed in on the debate. The term *vegan,* a contraction of *vegetarian,* dates from 1944. The Vegan Society describes its philosophy as a "way of living which seeks to exclude—as far as is possible and practical—all forms of exploitation of, and cruelty to, animals for food, clothing or any other purpose; and by extension, promotes the development and use of animal-free alternatives for the benefit of humans, animals, and the environment. In dietary terms it denotes the practice of dispensing with all products derived wholly or partly from animal" (Vegan Society 2010). Although most vegetarians consider honey to be an acceptable food, vegans in general eschew it for a variety of reasons, not the least of which is that taking honey from bees is viewed as exploitation or, even worse, enslavement and thus by definition cruel. Most vegetarians, however, do not view keeping bees as any more exploitative than keeping other forms of livestock. In fact, they often embrace honey as a healthier alternative to sucrose.

The question of whether bees are in fact livestock remains at the center of active debate by various and sundry groups, including the U.S. government. Before 2008, beekeepers did not qualify for crop insurance from the federal Risk Management Agency under any of its programs, including the Supplemental Revenue Assistance Payments Program, Livestock Indemnity Program, and Livestock Forage Disaster Program. In creating the Emergency Assistance for Livestock, Honey Bees, and Farm-Raised Fish Program, however, the 2008 Farm Bill for the first time recognized beekeepers as equivalent to producers of livestock (and farm-raised fish) at least in twenty-two states.

Honey and Health

Initially, honey was prized as one of very few sources of sweetness, but of late rather more has been ascribed to it. Those who read tabloid newspapers might believe that honey has remarkable curative properties, and the expectations of those who frequent health food stores may rise even higher. Over the centuries, honey has been implicated as a cure for everything from cancer to bedwetting. Aristotle touted its virtues as a wound treatment around 350 BCE, and three centuries later Dioscorides recommended honey for the treatment of ulcers. In contemporary times many of these claims have been dismissed as worthless folklore. Nutritionists have similarly been less than sanguine about its benefits. In 1996, for example, two authors in the *British Journal of Nutrition* traced the history of honey in preindustrial diets and concluded that, nutritionally, it is "little different from sugar," and any vitamin or mineral components are present in concentrations too low to be of any significance (Allsop and Miller 1996).

Such statements, however, ignore the spectacular biochemical diversity of honey. Nectars, like many other plant secretions, are biochemically diverse, and this diversity is reflected in honey when nectar is concentrated. Among other things, nectars can contain highly aromatic volatile compounds of various biosynthetic classes that play an important role in attracting pollinators and ensuring pollinator fidelity. In addition, to discourage nectar-eaters who are not pollinators, nectars also contain a variety of plant secondary metabolites, the principal function of which is repelling or deterring unwelcome floral visitors. These compounds are also potentially antibacterial. Antibacterial activity of honey is known to vary with floral source, most likely due to differences in content of plant secondary metabolites. More recent scientific studies under controlled conditions confirm honey's medicinal properties (Bogdanov et al. 2008). Honey has been shown to inhibit more than sixty species of bacteria (Molan 1992), and in 2008 the Food and Drug Administration approved the use of manuka honey from the manuka tree (*Leptospermum scoparium*), which grows in New Zealand, in the use of wound dressing to treat methicillin-resistant *Staphylococcus aureus,* the notorious flesh-eating bacterium MRSA. Honey also has demonstrable antifungal attributes.

One largely unexplored attribute of honey of potential dietary significance is its antioxidant content. Antioxidants are chemicals that protect against oxidative damage. Certain chemicals in the diet, ultraviolet light, and other environmental factors can generate toxic oxyradicals, forms of the oxygen molecule that cause DNA damage, and that damage can lead to a wide variety of age-related pathologies, including arthritis, strokes, and some cancers. Antioxidants, compounds that can reduce oxyradicals and thus counter their toxic effects, are commonly used to treat or lessen the incidence of these conditions. Honey has been successfully used for centuries as a treatment for cataracts and other eye ailments as well as for wounds, burns, ulcers, and other gastric ailments, all of which are conditions that toxic oxyradicals can generate. The use of honey to treat these conditions suggests that its antioxidant content, regardless of its chemical origins, may contribute to its therapeutic value.

In fact, honey contains many antioxidant chemicals, including some vitamins (e.g., vitamins A, C, and E) and enzymes (including catalase, which contributes to production of hydrogen peroxide). The antioxidant activity of any particular honey depends on its floral origins. According to one study, honeys can vary by more than an order of magnitude in antioxidant capacity (Frankel, Robinson, and Berenbaum 1998). At the high end are those that are darker in color, such as honey from buckwheat nectar. In general, antioxidant content is correlated with color intensity, an association not surprising in view of the fact that many pigments in honey, including the carotenoids, are powerful antioxidants.

The antioxidant properties of honey present possibilities for many applications other than as an ingredient in cookie recipes. Nicki Engeseth, a food chemist at the University of Illinois at Urbana-Champaign, has demonstrated that honey can prevent the browning caused by oxidation in ground meat products; other potential applications include the use of honey as an antibrowning agent in fruits and vegetables (Mckibben and Engeseth 2002). Honey inhibits the enzyme that causes oxidative browning in fruits and vegetables as well as or better than many commercial antioxidants such as sulfites, to which many people have allergies.

The antioxidants in honey may actually improve human health. Experimental studies show that honey in tea can improve the antioxidant capacity of the blood, preventing the formation of damaging lipid peroxides that can contribute to cerebrovascular and other diseases. The antioxidant content of honey compares favorably with that of some fruits and vegetables, but not everyone is happy about eating fruits and vegetables. Honey's extremely pleasing taste may influence those reluctant to ingest appropriate quantities of plant-derived antioxidants in the form of fruits and vegetables. At present, fifteen to thirty kilograms of sugar (thirty-three to sixty-six pounds) are eaten every year in the United States, and honey has much more to offer than sugar and many standard sweeteners (Phillips, Carlsen, and Blomhoff 2009). Refined sugar, corn syrup, and agave have virtually no antioxidant activity; raw cane sugar has low levels, but honey has an antioxidant capacity up to seven times greater. As Phillips, Carlsen, and Blomhoff conclude, "Based on an average intake of 130 g/day refined sugars and the antioxidant activity measured in typical diets, substituting alternative sweeteners could increase antioxidant intake an average of 2.6 mmol/day, similar to the amount found in a serving of berries or nuts." It doesn't hurt that the antioxidants in honey come in such a palatable package.

A Reader's Guide

There is no shortage of information on honey; thousands of books and tens of thousands of journal articles have been published. One source, though, is readily recognized as a honey bible of sorts; *Honey: A Comprehensive Survey* (1975), is out of print but available from many sources. The 608-page text was edited and largely written by Eva Crane, a legendary figure in the history of beekeeping. Trained as a nuclear physicist, she shifted her interest to bees and beekeeping after receiving a box of bees as a wedding gift in 1942, when, due to rationing because of World War II, sugar was in short supply. Until her death in 2007 at the age of ninety-five, she wrote prolifically and productively on subjects relating to honey bees and beekeeping, ultimately producing more than a hundred books, articles, and papers, many of which remain the definitive texts on their subjects.

Chapter 2

Cooking with Honey

*V*ern G. Milum was the first professor of apiculture—beekeeping—at the University of Illinois at Urbana-Champaign. Part of his job was to publish brochures for the public, extolling the virtues of honey. He also provided tips on cooking with honey. Among them, attributed to "one authority," is the general rule that "honey drizzled is better than honey poured, for a little gives just the sweetness desired and intensifies natural flavors, whereas a quantity of thick honey poured on a dish makes it too sweet." I don't know who actually said it, but it's a good rule to abide by.

To substitute honey for sugar, reduce the liquid in the recipe by a little (about one-fourth cup less liquid per cup of honey). Honey is also sweeter than sugar, so use only about three-fourths cup for every cup of sugar in a recipe. And honey is also a little acidic, so adding a little more baking soda (about one-half teaspoon per cup of honey) can counteract acidity. Unless you want to make honey cookies, honey muffins, or honey cake, it's best to mix honey with sugar or another kind of sweetener. Honey brings not only sweetness but also distinctive flavor and aroma. That's part of its appeal and also part of the reason many people are reluctant to cook with honey; cookies made with honey become honey cookies, cakes made with honey become honey cakes, and so on. Moreover, baked goods made with honey brown more quickly than those made with sugar and so should be cooked at lower temperatures.

In the kitchen, honey isn't quite as obedient as sugar. It can be difficult to store, measure, and pour. Under the right conditions, though, honey can keep for centuries. Room temperature is optimal. Many honeys also have a tendency to granulate, or crystallize. In some parts of the world crystallized honey is preferred to liquid honey, but in the United States most people are fans of the fluid state. The tendency to crystallize depends on the relative proportion of glucose to fructose; sugars higher in glucose, such as alfalfa or clover, are more prone to crystallize than those with proportionately less glucose, such as orange blossom. Because of its high fructose content, honey from the white tupelo (*Nyssa ogeche)* almost never crystallizes. Returning crystallized honey to its liquid state is a simple matter of gentle heating, either by placing the jar in a microwave oven and heating it for brief intervals or by placing the jar in a pot of water and gradually increasing the temperature.

In its liquid state, honey can be tricky to wrangle. Coating the measuring container with a little cooking oil will increase the likelihood that all measured quantities will leave the container on command. When mixing honey into a batter, pouring it in a steady stream makes blending easier.

Types of Honey

Given that it tastes good and is good for you, it's nice to know that honey can be enjoyed in many forms. It can be eaten raw in the comb or extracted and consumed in liquid form. The U.S. Department of Agriculture recognizes seven types of extracted honey based on color: water white, extra white, white, extra light amber, light amber, amber, and dark amber. Based on clarity, flavor, aroma, and absence of defects, honey is graded either A, B, C, or substandard. Honey can also be certified organic and certified kosher. It can be raw, strained, ultrafiltered, or heat-treated, and it can be whipped (or creamed) to achieve a smooth spreading consistency. In the United States, most honey is blended—mixed from a variety of floral sources and geographic locations to achieve a standard color and flavor. Monofloral honeys, however, which are derived primarily from single source, are enjoying increasing popularity. "Primarily" by convention means that more than 50 percent of the nectar used by bees to produce a particular honey was from a single floral source. The reason that monoflorals cannot be certifiably 100 percent from a single floral source is that bees may forage up to three miles from their home hive, and, despite everything a beekeeper might do to ensure repeated visits to a particular type of flower (e.g., placing hives in the middle of a large field, grove, or orchard of the target species), little can be done to keep the bees in the neighborhood once they begin foraging.

One reason for the growing interest in monofloral honeys is that each type offers a different honey-eating experience, a highly desirable objective for gourmets. Like wine, honeys vary with locality, year, and (human) producer (vintner/beekeeper). Thus, monoflorals, sometimes called honey varietals, offer a flavor palette that can brighten, accentuate, or counterbalance other food elements, particularly spicy ones. The award-winning Australian chef Skye Glyngell observed in *The Independent* on April 29, 2007, that "acacia is the perfect honey to pair with black truffles. Its flavour is delicate and absorbs easily the earthy, fragrant flavour of the truffles, and young crumbly Pecorino works alongside it perfectly." Or, the Tourist District of Laghi e Valli d'Ossola notes, "Chestnut honey is produced all over Italy in mountainous areas of medium altitude. Deep amber with reddish hints, its scent is penetrating and taste intense and pungent, almost bitter. Aromatic and decisive, it pairs well with rye bread and lard or aged cheeses." And in August 2006 *Gourmet Magazine* published a recipe for raspberry crème fraiche: "lush summer raspberries are framed by a rich crust and a cool, creamy layer that underlines their tart juiciness. A drizzling of warm lavender honey draws out a luxurious floral sweetness—put out the extra honey in a crock so everyone can add as much or as little as they like."

Although most honey sold in the United States is blended from multiple floral sources, particularly clover, American bees produce more than three hundred different varietal honeys. Some are distinctly regional. Honeys from the American South, for example, include tupelo, from the white tupelo (*Nyssa ogeche)* or the black tupelo (*Nyssa aquatica).* White tupelo honey, which almost never crystallizes, is highly prized for its unique delicate flavor. It is produced commercially only in northwest Florida. Tupelo trees produce flowers for only a two- to three-week period, and harvesting the honey in the remote swamps where the trees are found requires tremendous effort and intimate knowledge of the region. Another regionally distinct monofloral is lehua honey, produced only from nectar of the ohia lehua tree (*Metrosideros polymorpha*), which is restricted to the volcanic mountains of the islands in the Hawaiian archipelago. This unusual amber-colored honey is liquid when harvested from the beehive, but it quickly crystallizes and turns into a semi-solid upon standing.

It may take effort to locate varietal honeys, but they are certainly worth seeking out for anyone interested in the full range of the honey experience. Locally, they are sold at many farmers' markets, and a good fraction of the three hundred different types can be ordered over the Internet. One Internet source even customizes its varietal assortments to suit any occasion ("Bee Raw").

Although each varietal honey is unique and distinctive, there are general trends that can guide the selection of a particular monofloral for use in a particular recipe. Generally, darker honeys have stronger flavors. Buckwheat honey, for example, has a strong taste reminiscent of molasses; avocado has a caramelized flavor, and eucalyptus has a vaguely menthol essence. Among medium honeys are orange blossom, with citrus notes; fruity blueberry honey; and the slightly fruity, slightly buttery, slightly herbal tupelo honey. The light honeys tend to be the most broadly embraced. Clover and alfalfa, for example, are both sweet and flowery; sourwood has a licorice-like flavor; and fireweed from the Pacific Northwest, almost waterlike in color or lack thereof, is delicate and slightly fruity.

Unfortunately, the U.S. Department of Agriculture has no established standards for labeling honey varieties (only for honey quality), so unscrupulous beekeepers can label a honey as a monofloral regardless of the nectars that went into its production. Even worse, however, is the fact that honey can also be adulterated with comparative ease—contaminated with high-fructose corn syrup, pesticides, or worse. The sale of adulterated honey is big business; contaminated honey from China is often smuggled into the United States and relabeled as originating elsewhere. In 2009, Boa Zhong Zhang, a Chinese executive, pleaded guilty to "honey laundering" charges in the U.S. District Court in Seattle (Schneider 2008). With a partner, Chung Po Liu of Bellevue, Washington, Zhang was charged with trying to avoid $3.3 million in antidumping tariffs by planning to ship over $1.5 million worth of honey to Thailand and the Philippines and relabeling it to make it appear as if it originated in those countries. The best way to avoid adulterated honey is to purchase honey directly from a local beekeeper. Not only does it reduce the likelihood of being the victim of honey laundering but it also promotes beekeeping across the country.

About the Recipes in This Book

The recipes that follow come from around the world as well as from past decades, but all have been adapted for use in contemporary American kitchens and with respect for contemporary American sensitivities. One baklava recipe, for example, that originally included instructions for making phyllo from scratch, a lengthy and complicated process requiring art as much as culinary science, was modified so frozen phyllo pastry can be used. Abbreviations include C (cup), t (teaspoon), and T (tablespoon) and are given in nonmetric units throughout. Oven temperatures are given in degrees Fahrenheit.

Chapter 3

Drop Cookies

First-Prize Honey Hermits

This recipe is from the Culinary Honey Competition at the 1934 Illinois State Fair. Hermits constituted a separate competition category. Why they're called hermits isn't clear. The name might be because the cookies were originally baked individually rather than together as bars, although, ironically, later recipes do call for baking hermits in bar form. Another explanation is that the recipe originated with the Moravians, ethnic Protestant settlers in Pennsylvania well known for their spice cookies; Moravians were called Herrnhutter *in German or Dutch, which may have been contracted to "hermits" by English-speaking bakers.*

½ C butter
½ C sugar
½ C honey
1 egg
¾ C dates, chopped

¼ C candied pineapple, chopped
½ t cinnamon
½ t salt
1½ t baking soda
2 C flour

Cream butter, sugar, and honey. Beat egg and add to creamed mixture. Stir in chopped dates and pineapple. Mix and sift dry ingredients, and combine with creamed mixture. Drop dough by teaspoonful on greased cookie sheet and bake at 350 degrees 20–25 minutes.

YIELDS 2–3 DOZEN COOKIES.

Source: Adapted from the *Annual Report of the Illinois State Beekeepers Association,* 1934.

Honey Drop Cookies

½ C butter
½ C sugar
1 C honey
2 eggs, separated
2 T lemon juice with grated zest

3 C flour
1 t baking soda
granulated sugar (optional)
shredded coconut (optional)

Cream butter and gradually beat in sugar, honey, beaten yolks of 2 eggs, lemon juice, and grated zest. Beat egg whites until stiff and dry and fold into butter mixture. Sift flour with baking soda. Stir into butter-egg mixture. More flour may be added if needed to make a soft dough. Drop dough by teaspoonful onto a buttered cookie sheet; smooth tops of cookies, and bake at 350 degrees for 10–12 minutes, or until lightly browned. For a change, may be sprinkled with granulated sugar and coconut.

YIELDS 2–3 DOZEN COOKIES.

Honey Wafers

3 egg whites
½ C honey

1 C graham cracker crumbs
½ C chopped pecans

Beat egg whites in a large mixing bowl until stiff. Gradually beat in honey, stir in crumbs, and pecans. Drop dough by teaspoonful on well-greased cookie sheet. Bake at 300 degrees for 8 minutes, or until set and delicately browned.

YIELDS ABOUT 3 DOZEN WAFERS.
Source: Personal notes of Hermilda Listeman.

Pfeffernüsse

The name pfeffernüsse *translates literally to "pepper nuts" and refers, respectively, to the spicy taste and general shape of these traditional Christmas cookies from Germany.*

Cookies

½ C honey
½ C molasses or maple syrup
3 T butter
3 C flour
¾ t salt
¾ t baking powder
½ t ground cinnamon

¼ t ground cardamom
¾ t baking soda
½ t ground black pepper
½ t ground allspice
¼ t ground anise seed
1 egg

Heat honey and molasses or syrup over low heat in a small saucepan for about 10 minutes. Add butter, stir until melted; remove from heat and let cool. In a large bowl, sift together the dry ingredients. When honey mixture is lukewarm, whisk in the egg. Pour honey-egg mixture into the dry ingredients, mixing until well blended. The dough may be refrigerated to firm it up for easier rolling. Roll dough into small balls and bake on ungreased nonstick cookie sheets for 13–15 minutes, or until cookies hold their shape if tapped. Remove from pan and cool before frosting.

YIELDS 5–6 DOZEN SMALL COOKIES.

Frosting

1 egg white
2 t honey

½ t vanilla
1½ C powdered sugar

Whisk egg white, honey, and vanilla together until creamy. Sift powdered sugar over mixture and mix until smooth. Place a handful of cookies in small bowl, drizzle with few tablespoons of frosting, toss carefully until coated. Place cookies on a rack so icing can drip off. Repeat until all cookies are frosted. Let cookies dry before moving.

YIELDS 1½ C FROSTING.

Simple Honey Cookies

½ C butter, softened   2 C flour
½ C honey   2 t baking powder
1 egg, beaten   ½ t salt
2 T milk   1 C nuts (optional)

Cream together butter, honey, and egg. Beat until fluffy, then stir in milk. Sift flour before measuring; add salt and baking powder. Stir the dry ingredients into the butter-honey mixture, then add nuts. Drop by heaping teaspoonful onto a greased cookie sheet 2–3 inches apart. Bake at 350 degrees for 12–15 minutes, or until lightly browned.

YIELDS ABOUT 4 DOZEN COOKIES.

Honey-Lemon Pecan Snaps

½ C butter, softened   1½ t baking soda
½ C shortening   1 t ground cloves
1½ C sugar   1 t ground cinnamon
½ C honey   ½ t ground ginger
2 eggs   ¼ t nutmeg
2 T lemon juice   ½ t salt
zest of ½ lemon   1 C chopped pecans
4 C flour   additional sugar

Cream together butter, shortening, and sugar until fluffy. Add honey, eggs, lemon juice and zest and beat well. Combine dry ingredients and gradually stir into creamed mixture. Fold in pecans. Shape into 1-inch balls and roll in sugar. Place on ungreased cookie sheets. Bake at 350 degrees for 12–13 minutes, or until golden brown. Cool 2 minutes, then remove to wire racks.

YIELDS 4 DOZEN.

Glazed Greek Crescent Cookies

Based on a recipe on the website of Golden Blossom Honey, a company dating back to 1932. The honey is a blend of three varietal honeys: extra-white clover, sage buckwheat, and orange blossom.

1 C butter	1 t vanilla
¾ C sugar	4½ C flour
1 t grated orange zest	1 t baking powder
¼ C orange juice	½ t baking soda
2 T cognac	

Glaze

½ C water	⅔ C sugar
⅓ C Golden Blossom honey	1 C blanched almonds, chopped

Cream butter with sugar. Mix in orange zest, juice, cognac, and vanilla. Combine flour, baking powder, and baking soda, and then add to butter-sugar mixture a little at a time, stirring to combine after each addition. Spoon out dough with a tablespoon and shape each cookie into a crescent. Place on a lightly greased cookie sheet. Bake at 350 degrees for 10–15 minutes, or until lightly browned. Remove cookies and place on wire racks to cool.

As cookies cool, prepare glaze in a small saucepan. Mix together water, honey, and the remaining sugar. Heat to a gentle boil and continue to boil for 5 minutes. Dip cookies into the honey syrup, coat with chopped almonds, and allow to dry.

YIELDS APPROXIMATELY 50 COOKIES.

Honey Gems

3 T butter, melted
1½ C honey
1 C molasses
4 heaping t brown sugar
⅔ C water

¼ t vanilla
7½–8 C flour
1 t salt
1½ T baking soda
additional sugar (optional)

In a large bowl, combine butter, honey, molasses, brown sugar, water, and vanilla. Mix together dry ingredients and gradually add to butter mixture, stirring well to combine all ingredients. Drop by teaspoonful onto greased cookie sheet, or roll dough into 1-inch balls and roll in sugar to coat. Bake at 350 degrees for 9–10 minutes.

Source: Adapted from Mrs. C. C. Cleveland, Bartlett, in *The Cook County Cook Book,* 1912, page 95, Community Cookbook Collection of Hermilda Listeman (University of Illinois Library).

Honey Oatmeal Cookies

This recipe is a combination of the first- and second-prize-winning recipes from the 1934 Illinois State Fair Culinary Honey Competition. Buckwheat, a dark honey, is well suited to this recipe. Other dark honeys include avocado and tulip-poplar, which is dark in color but not as strong as other dark honeys.

1 C butter
½ C sugar
½ C dark honey
2 eggs, beaten
4 T buttermilk
1 t vanilla

2 C flour, sifted
1 t baking soda
1 t cinnamon
pinch of salt
2 C oatmeal
1 C raisins

Cream butter with sugar and honey. Stir in eggs, buttermilk, and vanilla. In a separate bowl, sift flour with baking soda, cinnamon, and salt. Stir flour mixture into butter mixture and combine well. Add oats and raisins. Drop dough by teaspoonful onto a greased cookie sheet. Bake at 400 degrees 10–15 minutes until browned.

YIELDS ABOUT 50 COOKIES.
Source: Adapted from the *Annual Report of the Illinois State Beekeepers Association,* 1934.

Honey Haystacks

1 C butter, softened	2½ C flour
1 C honey	1 C shredded coconut
2 eggs	¼ t cinnamon

Cream butter and ½ C honey; beat in eggs one at a time. Add flour gradually. Make balls of dough with heaping teaspoon and place on ungreased cookie sheet. Bake at 350 degrees for 5 minutes.

While cookies are baking, mix coconut, the remaining ½ C honey, and cinnamon in a small bowl. When cookies are done, remove from oven and allow them to cool slightly. Make a small depression in the center of each cookie, using a thumb or finger, and fill the cavity with some of the coconut mixture. Return cookie sheet to the oven to bake for another 5 minutes. Cool cookies on racks.

YIELDS ABOUT 40 COOKIES.

Source: Adapted from *American Honey Queen* recipe brochure, 1983, American Beekeeping Federation, Gainesville, Fla.

Staten Island Honey Cookies

In the mid-1970s, New York state ranked number one among eastern states in honey production, producing $7 million in honey and beeswax annually.

1 C butter, melted	2 t ginger
1 C honey	1½ t salt
½ C sugar	1 t baking soda
1 egg, beaten	1 t baking powder
4 C flour	½ t cloves
2 t cinnamon	

Combine melted butter, honey, and sugar; let cool slightly before adding egg. Combine dry ingredients and add all at once to butter mixture. Beat for 20 strokes. Allow batter to cool until dough can be handled. Shape dough into 1½-inch balls, place on greased cookie sheet 2 inches apart, and bake at 350 degrees for 15 minutes.

YIELDS 4 DOZEN COOKIES.

Honey Chocolate Chip Cookies

Although the original "Nestlé's toll house cookie," dating back to 1934 at the Toll House Inn of Whitman, Mass., included brown and white sugars but not honey, the Wikipedia entry for "chocolate chip cookie" states that "almost all baking-oriented cookbooks will contain at least one type of [this] recipe," so here it is.

1 C butter, room temperature	1 t vanilla
1 C brown sugar	3½ C flour
2 eggs	2 t baking soda
⅓ C honey	1 (6 oz) package semisweet chocolate chips

Cream butter and sugar together; stir in eggs, honey, and vanilla. Stir in flour and baking soda; add chocolate chips. Chill dough for several hours. Drop dough by tablespoon onto ungreased cookie sheet and bake at 350 degrees for 10–12 minutes.

YIELDS 60 COOKIES.

Honey Peanut Butter Cookies

Another cookie staple that partners well with honey.

½ C butter	½ t salt
1 C peanut butter	2½ C flour
1 C sugar	1½ t baking soda
1 C honey	1 t baking powder
2 eggs, beaten	

Cream together butter, peanut butter, and sugar, beating until smooth. Stir in honey, eggs, and salt. Mix together dry ingredients and add to butter mixture. Chill dough for several hours. Drop dough by teaspoonful onto cookie sheet; flatten with a flour-dipped fork and crisscross the top. Bake at 375 degrees for 8 minutes.

YIELDS APPROXIMATELY 48 COOKIES.

Honeydoodles

A popular sugar cookie that easily accommodates honey.

½ C (1 stick) unsalted butter

1 C sugar, plus 3 T

1 egg

1½ t honey

¼ t vanilla

1¾ C flour

1½ t baking powder

1 t baking soda

⅛ t salt

¾ t cinnamon

Combine butter and 1 cup of the sugar and beat until fluffy. Beat in the egg, honey, and vanilla. Combine flour, baking powder, baking soda, salt, and ¼ t cinnamon; slowly beat dry ingredients into the butter mixture. In a small bowl, combine the remaining 3 T sugar and ½ t cinnamon. Form the dough into 1-inch balls. Roll the balls in the sugar-cinnamon mixture. Place the balls 2 inches apart on cookie sheets. Bake at 375 degrees for 10–12 minutes, or until golden brown and slightly cracked on the top. Transfer cookies to a wire rack to cool.

Yoyo Biscuits

An Australian favorite.

1 C butter, softened	1 t vanilla
1 C brown sugar	3½ C flour
2 eggs	2 t baking soda
⅓ C honey	

Icing

1 C powdered sugar	2 T lemon juice
1 T unsalted butter, softened	

Cream butter with brown sugar until smooth; beat in eggs. Mix in honey and vanilla. Sift together flour and baking soda and add to creamed mixture. Refrigerate 1 hour (or overnight). Form dough into balls approximately 1 inch in diameter and place onto ungreased cookie sheet. Flatten with fork, making a crisscross pattern. Bake at 350 degrees for 10–12 minutes.

While cookies are baking, make icing by mixing all ingredients until smooth. After cookies have cooled, spread icing mixture on the base of half of the cookies and top with remaining cookies to make sandwiches.

South African Honey Lemon Biscuits

Hugh Robertson, a University of Illinois at Urbana-Champaign entomology professor, grew up in South Africa and remembers these cookies. Two races of honey bees can be found in South Africa, and both are world-renowned, albeit for different reasons. Found in the Highveld, Apis mellifera scutellata *is the notorious "killer bee," the race introduced to Brazil in 1957 that escaped and colonized much of the Western Hemisphere, including the southern United States. South of Bloemfontein is* Apis mellifera capensis, *a race unique in its ability to reproduce parthenogenetically—that is, without benefit of mating. Both races make delicious honey.*

7 T unsalted butter, softened
½ C sugar
⅓ C light honey
2 t grated lemon zest
½ t lemon extract

1 egg
1¾ C flour
1 t baking powder
½ t salt
¼ C plain fat-free yogurt

Glaze

1 C powdered sugar
2 T fresh lemon juice

2 t grated lemon zest

Cream together butter and sugar; mix in honey, lemon zest, lemon extract, and egg. Add in flour, baking powder, and salt, alternating with yogurt. Drop by teaspoonful onto greased cookie sheet; bake at 350 degrees for 12 minutes, or until lightly browned.

Place glaze ingredients in a small bowl and stir until blended. Drizzle over cooled cookies.

Brunscrackers (Swedish Brown Cookies)

Honey is an integral part of Swedish culture. Beekeeping, however, is not easy in Sweden. In addition to long winters and the irascible nature of the "dark bee of Northern Europe," Apis mellifera mellifera, *there's also the challenge brought to the attention of the public in May 2009 by the Swedish National Association of Beekeepers: brown bears that have developed a taste for honey.*

1 C butter
1 C sugar plus additional
   for topping
2 T honey

1 t vanilla
2 C flour
1 t baking soda

Cream butter with sugar and honey, then add vanilla. Mix together flour and baking soda, and then add to the wet ingredients to make a soft dough. Scoop dough by teaspoon, form into balls, roll in granulated sugar, and place on the cookie sheet. Flatten the dough balls with the bottom of a drinking glass dipped in sugar. Bake at 300 degrees for 10 minutes, or until cookies are light brown. Remove from cookie sheet and cool on a wire rack.

Sweet Potato Marshmallow Cookies

A recipe I developed in a futile effort to win the Louisiana Sweet Potato Commission's Sweet Rewards recipe contest.

1½ C all-purpose flour
1½ t baking soda
1½ t baking powder
½ t salt
½ t nutmeg
½ t cinnamon
½ C unsalted butter, softened

¾ C light honey
1 large egg
1 C well-mashed sweet potatoes
½ t vanilla
¼ C orange juice
½ C pecans, chopped
1 C miniature marshmallows

Sift flour, baking powder, baking soda, salt, cinnamon, and nutmeg into a bowl. In a separate large bowl, cream the butter and honey. Add egg; stir in sweet potato, vanilla, and orange juice. Slowly add dry mixture, stirring after each addition. Fold in pecans. Drop batter by ice cream scoop onto buttered cookie sheets. Gently insert 3 marshmallows into each cookie. Bake at 400 degrees for 12 to 15 minutes, or until slightly browned. Cool on racks.

Chapter 4
Bar Cookies and Brownies

Anna's Swedish Honey Leckerli

This recipe is from Illinois artist Christina Nordholm's Great Grandma Anna.

⅔ C clover honey
⅔ C sugar
1 T kirsch (cherry brandy) or
   triple sec liqueur
2½ t cinnamon
¼ t cloves

grated peel of 1 large lemon
¼ C each finely chopped candied
   lemon peel and candied orange peel
⅔ C sliced almonds
2¼ C unbleached flour (have more
   in reserve to add as needed)

Glaze

1½ C powdered sugar
⅛ t vanilla extract

3 T water

Position 2 oven racks in the center third of the oven. Heat oven to 350 degrees. Generously grease 2 baking sheets, 10 by 14 inches or larger. In a medium-sized saucepan, combine the honey, sugar, and kirsch over medium heat, stirring until the sugar completely dissolves and the mixture is hot but not boiling. Remove from heat and add cinnamon, cloves, grated lemon peel, candied peels, and almonds. Stir until completely incorporated.

Add 2¼ C flour gradually to the warm mixture in the pan; stir vigorously after each addition. The mixture will become very stiff. When all flour has been added, if the mixture feels sticky and too soft to roll, stir or knead in a bit more flour but add as little as you can to be able to handle it. Set the dough aside to cool until barely warm.

Sprinkle a work surface generously with flour. Divide the dough in half. Roll each half into an 8½ by 13-inch rectangle, frequently running a spatula under the dough and re-flouring the work surface. As needed, also dust the top of the dough and the rolling pin with flour. Work quickly and lightly. To transfer dough, pick up the rolled-out dough by folding it gently over the rolling pin and place on a prepared baking sheet. Repeat with the second half of the dough. Prick dough lightly all over with a fork.

Put baking sheets on racks in the center third of the oven; bake for 15 minutes. Switch the positions of the pans and/or rotate halfway through the baking time to ensure even browning. Do not over-bake, as cookies will become too hard. As soon as you remove them from the oven, carefully loosen the cookies from the baking sheet by running a spatula under the dough rectangles, easing them from the pan. Let them cool enough to handle, then transfer the rectangles to a cutting board and cut away any uneven dry edges. With a serrated knife, score into 1 by 2½-inch rectangles but *don't cut completely through the surface.* Carefully return the scored rectangles to the baking sheets before glazing.

In a small saucepan, stir together the powdered sugar, vanilla, and 3 T water until thoroughly blended. Bring the mixture to a boil, stirring for 20 to 30 seconds until smooth, very fluid, and translucent. Divide the glaze evenly between the two sheets of cookies by pouring over the rectangles and *quickly* spreading the glaze over the entire surface. Let stand until the glaze sets and turns white again, about an hour. To separate cookies bend the rectangles to break apart or cut through the score marks. Let stand until the glaze is dry and hard. Will keep for up to 3 weeks or more in an airtight container.

YIELDS 50 TO 60 1 BY 2½-INCH BARS.

Honey Butterscotch Brownies

½ C butter	1½ C flour
½ C brown sugar, packed	½ t salt
½ C honey	1 t baking powder
1 egg, beaten	½ C chopped nuts (optional)
1 t vanilla	

Cream together butter, brown sugar, and honey; stir in egg and vanilla. Mix together dry ingredients and combine with butter mixture. Stir in nuts. Pour batter into a buttered 9 by 9-inch pan. Bake at 350 degrees for 25–30 minutes; don't overbake. Remove from oven, cut into bars, and allow to cool.

Swiss Leckerli

From Art Zangerl, research associate in the Department of Entomology at the University of Illinois at Urbana-Champaign, whose family roots extend back to Neuchatel, Switzerland.

16 oz honey
1½ C sugar
pinch of cloves
1½ T cinnamon
½ t nutmeg
3½ oz each minced candied
   orange and lemon peel

6 oz ground almonds
zest of 1 lemon
4 C flour
1½ t baking powder
kirsch (about 2–3 T)

Glaze

⅓ C powdered sugar

3–5 T kirsch or water

Mix honey, sugar, cloves, cinnamon, and nutmeg in a pan; heat slowly until sugar dissolves, then remove from heat. Add candied orange and lemon peel, almonds, and lemon zest; stir until mixed. Add kirsch, flour, and baking powder and stir vigorously to combine. Knead on a table to form a soft dough, adding more kirsch if necessary. Roll dough out ¼-inch thick on the back of 2 greased baking sheets. Bake at 425 degrees for about 15–20 minutes in the center of the preheated oven (over-baking will make them very hard). While cookies are baking, mix confectioner's sugar with kirsch or water. Glaze cookies immediately after removing from the oven. While still warm, cut into 2-inch squares.

YIELDS 3 TO 4 DOZEN BARS.

Caramel Honey Crisps

½ C butter
½ C honey
25 caramels, unwrapped

8 C cornflakes
1 C sliced almonds (optional)

Combine butter and honey in saucepan, bring to boil. Boil 1 minute and turn off heat. Stir in caramels until they have melted and sauce is smooth. Measure cornflakes into large greased bowl. Pour caramel sauce over cornflakes; stir until mixture completely coats flakes. Stir in almonds. Turn mixture into a greased 9 by 13-inch baking pan. Bake at 350 degrees about 7 minutes. Remove from oven; let cool and cut into squares.

YIELDS ABOUT 48 SQUARES.
Source: Personal notebooks of Hermilda Listeman.

Caramel Pecan Bars

Crust
1 C butter, softened
½ C brown sugar

3 C flour
1 egg, beaten

Filling
3 C pecan halves or
   chopped pieces
¾ C butter

¾ C brown sugar
¼ C whipping cream
½ C honey

For crust, mix butter, brown sugar, flour, and egg until blended. Press evenly into 15 by 10 by ¾-inch jelly-roll pan. Bake at 350 degrees for 15 minutes.

For filling, sprinkle pecan halves evenly over crust. In large, heavy saucepan melt butter; add honey and brown sugar; stir to dissolve. Bring mixture to a boil over medium high heat and let boil for 5–7 minutes, or until mixture reaches a rich caramel color. Remove from heat and stir in whipping cream. Combine thoroughly. Pour caramel mixture over pecans. Bake at 350 degrees for 15 minutes, or until done; cool.

YIELDS 4 DOZEN BARS.

Almond-Fruit Diamonds

The "favorite cookie for 1980":

Crust

3 C flour

⅛ t salt

1½ C butter, divided

1 C sugar, divided

2 eggs

½ t grated lemon peel

Topping

½ C honey

2 T heavy cream

1 t vanilla

1 C sliced almonds

¾ C red and green candied cherries

Preheat oven to 350 degrees. Adjust oven rack to lower third of oven. Grease 15½ by 10½-inch jelly-roll pan.

Combine flour and salt in large bowl. Beat 1C butter and ½ C sugar in large mixing bowl at medium speed. Beat in eggs and lemon peel until mixture is light and fluffy. Gradually beat in dry ingredients. Press dough evenly into prepared pan, making a ¼-inch high rim. Bake 25–30 minutes until top is lightly brown and dough is firm to the touch. Five minutes before crust is done, melt remaining ½ C butter in saucepan, add honey, remaining ½ C sugar, cream, and vanilla. Heat to boiling, then boil, stirring for 5 minutes. Stir in almonds and fruit. Pour over crust. Bake 10 minutes more. Cool. Cut into 2 by 1¼-inch diamonds.

YIELDS 52 COOKIES.
Source: Personal notebooks of Hermilda Listeman.

Honey Lemon-Slice Cookie Bars

1 C brown sugar, firmly packed
2 C sifted flour
½ C butter + 2 T
1 C shredded or flaked coconut

1 C pure honey
¼ C lemon juice
3 eggs, beaten unmercifully

Blend together brown sugar, flour, butter, and coconut. Pat ⅔ of mixture into an ungreased 9-inch square pan. In small saucepan, cook together honey, 2 T butter, lemon juice, and eggs, stirring constantly until mixture thickens. Cool and spread over coconut mixture in pan. Sprinkle remainder of coconut mixture over top. Bake at 350 degrees for 40 minutes. Cut in 1½-inch squares and cool in pan or rack.

YIELDS 3 DOZEN BARS.
Source: Personal notebooks of Hermilda Listeman, with the note "from the Gourmet Co-op."

Honey Nut Brownies

Note: If the brownies will be eaten immediately, use a combination of ½ C honey and ½ C brown sugar.

¼ C butter
2 oz bitter chocolate
1 C honey
2 eggs, beaten

½ C flour
½ t baking powder
1 C chopped nuts

Melt butter and chocolate together, then stir in honey (see Note). Add eggs and stir to combine well. Sift flour and baking powder and stir into chocolate mixture. Add nuts. Bake at 300 degrees for 45 minutes. Pack brownies away in jar or bread box. Before serving, cut in strips about ½-inch wide and 2 inches long. Roll in powdered sugar if desired.

Source: Adapted from Vern Milum, University of Illinois Extension Service mimeographed bulletin, 1929.

First-Prize Honey Date Bars

This recipe was a prizewinner at the 1934 Illinois State Fair Honey Culinary Competition. The recipes for that event were published without attribution and often (as in the case of this recipe) without instructions. A handwritten note on the recipe indicates that "second and third prizes were Kellogs [sic] Honey Date Bars."

2 eggs	¼ t salt
¼ C honey	½ T baking powder
¼ C sugar	1¼ C dates, chopped
⅔ C flour	¾ C nuts, chopped

Beat eggs well and mix in honey and sugar. Sift flour with salt and baking powder and add to egg mixture. Stir in dates and nuts. Spread in a greased 11 by 15-inch jelly-roll pan. Bake at 350 degrees for 15–25 minutes. Cut into strips ½ inch wide and 3 inches long.

Source: Adapted from the *Annual Report of the Illinois State Beekeepers Association,* 1934.

Apricot Bars

½ C butter	1 t salt
1½ C brown sugar, packed	1 t baking powder
½ C honey	1 t cinnamon
zest of 1 lemon	6 oz dried apricots, chopped
3 eggs	1 C chopped or slivered almonds
1¾ C flour	

Lemon Glaze

¾ C powdered sugar	1 T lemon juice

Cream butter, sugar, honey, and lemon zest; beat in eggs. In a separate bowl, combine dry ingredients. Mix into creamed mixture and stir until thoroughly blended. Fold in almonds and apricots. Spread into 15 by 10 by 1-inch baking pan and bake at 350 degrees for 20–25 minutes. Cut into bars.

To make the glaze, mix sifted powdered sugar with lemon juice. Pour over cooled bars.

YIELDS ABOUT 50 BARS.

Beehives

A recipe translated by Martin Hauser, a Ph.D. graduate in entomology at the University of Illinois at Urbana-Champaign and originally from Germany.

½ C butter
1 egg yolk
4 T honey
⅓ C sugar
½ C ground hazelnuts
1⅔ C flour

1 t cinnamon
8 T rose-hip jam
a few drops of lemon juice
1 package agar-agar powder
powdered sugar for decoration

Mix butter, egg yolk, 1 T honey, sugar, nuts, flour, and cinnamon; refrigerate for 45 minutes. Roll dough flat (about ¼ inch thick) and cut 20 rounds approximately 1¾ inches in diameter, and 10 rounds a little more than an inch in diameter. Make hollow rings by cutting the centers out of all the small disks and 10 of the large disks. Place dough on baking paper. Bake at 350 degrees for 18 minutes. While dough is baking, mix the remaining honey, rose-hip jam, and lemon juice with the agar-agar powder. To assemble beehives, use a large disk for the bottom, and stack with rings. Fill the centers with the honey mixture; decorate with powdered sugar.

YIELDS APPROXIMATELY 10 BEEHIVES.

Really Rich Baklava

This recipe comes from Tugrul Giray, a University of Illinois at Urbana-Champaign bee biologist originally from Turkey and now living in Puerto Rico. As he describes it, "I had to first experiment and try this recipe at home. It is delicious! Definitely a diet food for gaining weight. I guess we can call it 'Baklava Heavy' or 'Non-light Baklava.'"

Note: Afyon cream (from Afyon Province, and reputed to be the most famous in Turkey, is prepared with water buffalo milk) will go on top of the baklava before serving. The first stage of this recipe needs to occur 36–48 hours before serving.

Topping
1 qt heavy cream

Syrup
½ C orange blossom honey   3 C water
2½ C sugar   1 t lemon juice

Filling
2–3 C walnut halves   ½ t cinnamon (optional)
1 T flavorful honey

Pastry
1-lb package phyllo sheets   1 stick butter (or more as needed)

Simmer heavy cream in a wide container (a deep stainless-steel pan is preferable) on low heat, stirring more or less continuously for 1 hour. Pour the thickened heavy cream in a tray (about ⅓ inch thick). Let cool to room temperature, cover with a layer of plastic wrap or waxed paper to prevent oxidation or color change, and refrigerate for 36–48 hours until it is solid and can be cut with a butter knife and served with a spatula.

To make the syrup: Mix orange blossom honey, sugar, and water; bring to a boil and let simmer for 30–40 minutes. Add lemon juice. Mix. Remove any foam or froth that may appear on the surface with a spoon or ladle. Leave this honey-sugar syrup to cool to room temperature on the kitchen counter.

To make the filling: Measure 2–3 C shelled walnut halves. Smash the walnuts to a granulate form by placing them inside a nylon bag and hitting the bag with a rolling pin or the bottom of the honey jar. Mix the tablespoon of flavorful honey (such as buckwheat honey) with the walnuts. This somewhat sticky mixture will go inside the baklava. Add a little zest or cinnamon to the mix if desired.

To assemble the pastry: Open a 1-pound package of phyllo sheets and prepare it on a table. Spread a large baking pan (about the size of a sheet of phyllo) with melted unsalted or sweet-cream butter. Melt the butter in a mug, either in a pan of simmering water or the microwave at 50 percent power, for a minute or so. The idea is to melt, not burn, the butter. Place 2 sheets of phyllo in the baking pan and brush with the melted butter. Repeat, melting another stick of butter if needed until about half the sheets have been used. Spread half the filling on this layer. Continue layering the phyllo and spreading butter until a quarter of the phyllo remains. Spread the rest of the filling on this layer. Continue layering phyllo sheets and spreading butter until all the sheets are used. By this point you generally will use ¾ to 1 pound of butter.

To bake: Preheat the oven to 350 degrees. While the oven is heating, cut the baklava pieces with a sharp knife, 5 cuts one way and 5 the other. This results in a baklava shape in round baking pans, squares in square baking pans, and rectangles in rectangular baking pans. Place the baklava pie into the preheated oven. Bake for 45–50 minutes. Raise the temperature to 375 and bake another 15 minutes or so. The idea is to bake the baklava to a golden-orange color.

To serve: Spoon the cool syrup on the baklava as soon as the baklava comes from the oven; it will make a sizzling sound as it "drinks" the honey syrup. Continue adding spoonfuls of syrup evenly over the baklava pieces as the syrup, likely all that has been prepared, soaks in. Some will remain around the baklava in the pan. Take care not to overdo the syrup. The warm baklava is now ready to serve. Place 1–3 pieces on a dessert plate and cover with Afyon cream.

Baagh-lava

Baklava, or its many variants, is a pastry that is popular throughout the Middle East. This is a modification of an Iranian version sent by Saber Miresmailli, a postdoctoral student in the Department of Entomology at the University of Illinois at Urbana-Champaign. The dish is traditionally served on Nowruz, the Iranian New Year's celebration, which falls on the first day of spring.

Filling
4 C almonds, blanched
   and ground
3 C confectioner's sugar

2 t ground cardamom
pinch of salt

Pastry
nonstick cooking spray
1 lb frozen phyllo sheets
   (ca. 20), thawed

1 T water

Syrup
1½ C wildflower honey
½ C water (rose water if available)

1 t lemon juice
2 pinches cardamom

Topping
½ C chopped pistachios

Preheat oven to 400 degrees. Spray a rimmed 13 by 9 by 1-inch baking sheet or jelly-roll pan with nonstick cooking spray. Combine nuts, sugar, and cardamom in a bowl. Lay phyllo sheets on the counter and cover with a damp towel. Place 1 sheet in the pan, spray with cooking spray, and cover with another sheet, repeating the procedure until about half the sheets are assembled. Spread the nut and sugar mixture evenly over the base of phyllo sheets. Resume spraying and layering the sheets until the entire package has been used. Trim the ends of sheets that overhang the pan. With a sharp knife, cut parallel lines through the pastry from top to bottom, creating diamond shapes. Bake 30–35 minutes or until golden brown. Remove from oven and cool for 10–15 minutes.

While pastry is baking, make honey syrup. In a saucepan on medium heat stir together honey and water, then mix in lemon juice and cardamom. Bring to boil and simmer for 20–25 minutes. Cool. Pour honey evenly over pastry and cool completely. Top with chopped pistachios if desired.

Brownie Muffins with Honeyed Cream Cheese

This is an adaptation of a recipe by Erin Renouf Mylroie, a finalist in a recipe contest that featured ingredients representing the entrant's home state, and honey certainly represents Utah. The state calls itself the Beehive State, a skep appears on the state seal, and at one point Utah was known as Deseret, a Mormon term for honey bee. Migratory beekeeping (the practice of moving bees to provide pollination service to crops) began with Utah legend Nephi Miller at the start of the twentieth century. Utah honey, produced in a desert climate, tends to have a low moisture content.

1 egg	3 T unsweetened cocoa
½ C sugar	¼ C chocolate chips
½ t vanilla	(semisweet or white)
¼ C buttermilk	¼ C strawberry cream cheese
4 T butter, melted	1 T honey
⅓ C flour plus 1 T	6 large strawberries, sliced in half

Beat together egg, sugar, vanilla, buttermilk, and butter. Stir in ⅓ C flour and cocoa.

Place 1 T flour in a small bowl; add chocolate chips and stir to coat. Add chips to brownie batter. Grease and flour mini muffin pans or use muffin liners. Pour brownie batter into pan, filling each cup ⅓ full. Bake at 350 degrees for 15–18 minutes. Invert pan and let brownies cool on rack. Combine cream cheese and honey in a small bowl and beat until fluffy. Top warm brownie muffins with 1 T cream cheese mixture and a strawberry slice. Serve immediately.

YIELDS 12 BROWNIES.

Chapter 5

Rolled Cookies

Aachener Nussprinten (Spiced Bread Cookies with Nuts)

Printen are the traditional cookies of Aachen, Germany. This recipe was contributed by Britta Demberg, a friend of Nils Cordes.

¾ C honey	½ t cinnamon
⅓ C brown sugar	1 T brown sugar
3 T butter	2½ C flour
1 egg, beaten	½ T hazelnuts or almonds (optional)
zest of 1 lemon	chocolate for glaze (optional)

Gently heat honey, sugar, and butter to dissolve. Let mixture cool, then add egg, lemon zest, cinnamon, brown sugar, and flour, combining thoroughly. Let batter rest in a cool place for 1 hour. Roll ¼ inch thick and cut into strips; place strips on a greased baking sheet. Decorate the cookies with halved hazelnuts or almonds. Bake at 350–370 degrees for 15–18 minutes. Glaze with melted chocolate. The printen can be stored for a long time. To soften, store with a slice of apple but be careful of mold.

Honey Crisp Wafers

This is the second-prize recipe from the 1934 Illinois State Fair Culinary Honey Competition; honey crisp wafers were in their own competition category.

½ C butter	1 T lemon juice
⅓ C sugar	2½ C flour
1 egg	3½ t baking powder
1 C honey	¼ t salt

Cream butter and sugar; add unbeaten egg and beat well. Add honey and lemon juice; sift flour with baking powder and salt and add to mixture. Stir to combine ingredients thoroughly. Roll dough thin and cut. Bake at 350 degrees for approximately 10 minutes, until nicely browned.

Source: Adapted from the *Annual Report of the Illinois State Beekeepers Association*, 1934.

Honey Ginger Snaps

Another recipe from the 1934 Illinois State Fair Culinary Honey Competition.

½ C molasses	1 T ginger
½ C dark honey	4 C flour
½ C butter	1 t baking soda

Mix molasses, honey, and butter; add ginger and set over low heat and stir until butter is melted. Remove from heat and stir in 4 C flour sifted with baking soda. Turn out dough onto lightly floured counter and knead dough until smooth; refrigerate overnight. Roll dough as thin as possible and cut into circles. Bake at 350 degrees for 15 minutes.

Southern Honey Pecan Cookies

To capture the essence of the South, tupelo honey, a monofloral produced commercially only in northwest Florida, would be a good choice.

½ C butter, softened	½ C whole-wheat flour
½ C sugar	2 t baking powder
1 egg, beaten	½ t salt
½ C honey	¾ C pecans, chopped
1½ C all-purpose flour	

Cream butter in bowl, gradually adding sugar and beating until light and fluffy. Add egg and honey, and mix well. Sift flour, baking powder, and salt in a medium bowl. Add dry ingredients to creamed mixture, stirring well. Add pecans and mix well. Shape dough into a roll 1½ inches in diameter. Wrap in waxed paper or plastic wrap and refrigerate overnight.

Remove dough from refrigerator, and cut into ¼-inch slices. Place on lightly greased cookie sheets. Bake at 375 degrees for 10–15 minutes, or until lightly browned. Remove from cookie sheets and cool on wire racks

YIELDS 5½ DOZEN COOKIES.

Oma's Pflastersteine (Cobblestones)

This recipe is from Janet Sperling, whose husband, Felix Sperling, is an entomologist at the University of Alberta, Edmonton. "These cookies are Eastern European Christmas cookies," she notes, "and are always popular with kids who are looking for a substantive treat. My mother-in-law (Oma to my kids) 'cures' the cookies for at least two weeks in an airtight tin but it's hard to keep the cookies hidden that long in my house. Most of the monofloral honey in stores in Alberta is clover honey, although there are producers of canola honey but it's rarely marketed as monofloral (it crystallizes very quickly). The majority of the honey we use is mixed clover, alfalfa and canola and is considered 'white honey.'"

⅔ C honey
⅔ C brown sugar
1 C butter
½ C marmalade
1 t cinnamon
½ t cloves

⅔ C ground almonds
1 egg
2½ C flour
3 t baking powder
½ C cocoa

In a saucepan, bring honey, sugar, and butter to a boil. Remove from heat. Add marmalade (10 g mixed peel in the original recipe). Add cinnamon, cloves, almonds, and egg. In a separate bowl, mix flour, baking powder, and cocoa. Add liquid to flour mix and stir. Roll out into a fairly thick slab and cut with a large cookie cutter. Bake at 375 degrees for 15 minutes, until the dough is slightly brown; avoid overcooking. Cool, then ice with a bit of powdered sugar mixed with lemon juice.

Spiced Honey Cakes (Leckerli)

"A favorite cookie from Switzerland." *You'll notice the ingredients are similar to the recipes included in the Bar Cookies section, but the preparation technique is a bit different.*

1¼ C sifted flour
2 t cinnamon
1 t ground cloves
½ C honey
½ C sugar

1 C grated or firmly ground almonds
½ t grated lemon zest
1½ T lemon juice
¼ C brandy or kirsch
⅓ C chopped candied lemon peel

Glaze
1 C water

½ C sugar

Sift together flour, cinnamon, and cloves. Simmer honey and sugar until sugar dissolves. Remove from heat; add almonds, lemon zest and juice, and brandy; mix well. Add flour mixture, mix until smooth. Stir in candied peel. Chill 1 hour. On floured board, roll out dough into a rectangle 10 by 12 inches and ¼ inch thick. Cut into 24 cookies. Place on well-floured cookie sheet, cover, and let stand overnight.

To make glaze, combine water and sugar in saucepan, cook to 220 degrees. When done, syrup mixture is grainy and becomes a little cloudy when rubbed against the pan.

Preheat oven to 350 degrees. Transfer cookies to greased cookie sheet. Bake 10–12 minutes, or until very delicately browned. Place on wire racks while hot and brush several times with glaze. Cool. Store cookies in an airtight container for 2–4 weeks to mellow.

YIELDS 2 DOZEN CAKES.
Source: Personal notebooks of Hermilda Listeman.

Lebkuchen (Honey Spice Cake)

"A spice cake recipe from Nuremberg, Germany, that goes back six hundred years and is a forerunner of gingerbread."

4 C flour	2 eggs
1 t cinnamon	¾ C sugar
¼ t ground cloves	¾ C candied orange peel
¼ t ginger	1 C blanched almonds, chopped fine
½ t salt	¾ C honey
½ t baking powder	candied cherries for garnish (optional)

Egg White Glaze

1 C sifted confectioner's sugar	1 t lemon juice
2 egg whites	

Sift flour together with spices, salt, and baking powder. Beat eggs until thick and creamy, then gradually beat in the sugar. Stir in 1 C of the flour mixture and add candied fruit. Mix almonds and honey together and stir in 1 C flour mixture. Now combine the egg dough and honey dough. Sprinkle a board with flour and knead the dough to combine. Finally, knead in remaining flour mixture. Take half the dough and roll ½ inch thick. Cut squares into 1 by 3-inch bars, or use a cookie cutter. Place on greased cookie sheets. Bake at 400 degrees for 10–12 minutes, or until cookies are golden brown. Lift from cookie sheets to cake racks and cool. Glaze when cold.

To make glaze, combine ingredients in a bowl and beat with electric beater for 5 minutes. Using a pastry brush, coat each cookie, then garnish with candied cherries. Age cookies between sheets of waxed paper in airtight containers for several weeks before serving.

Source: Personal notebooks of Hermilda Listeman.

Radtke Family Lebkuchen

"From Mildred Radtke, whose recipe won first prize in a contest sponsored by the Hermann, Mo., Advertiser Courier in 1986. This recipe, brought from Germany, has been in the Radtke family for four generations. Make the dough the weekend after Thanksgiving to get ready for Christmas. It can be refrigerated for as long as six months."

Cookie

2 C nuts (pecans)
2 C chopped dates
2 C raisins
2 T orange peel
2¾ C dark-brown sugar
1 C (2 sticks) butter, softened
1 C dark honey
¼ C brandy (or bourbon)
almond, pecan, or walnut halves,
   optional

3 eggs
1 t star anise steeped
   in 1 T boiling water
2 t baking soda
1 t cinnamon
1 t ground ginger
½ t ground nutmeg
5–6 C flour

Glaze

2 T milk
1 T butter, melted

3 drops vanilla
confectioner's sugar

Grind nuts, dates, raisins, and orange peel in a food processor or grinder. Cream brown sugar and butter with electric mixer. Add honey, brandy, and eggs. Mix well. Add star anise water and the ground nut and fruit mixture. Sift together baking soda, cinnamon, ginger, nutmeg, and flour. Gradually add dry ingredients to honey mixture; mix until a stiff dough is formed. Put dough in glass or earthenware bowl, cover tightly, and let age in refrigerator for 2 weeks or longer. When ready to bake, roll dough out ¼ inch thick on a heavily floured board. Dough is very sticky; it must be rolled in batches; return remaining dough to refrigerator. Cut dough into oblong bars, and transfer to a greased cookie sheet. Bake at 325 degrees for 15 minutes. Remove to wire racks and cool before glazing.

Prepare glaze: Combine milk, butter, vanilla, and enough sugar to make a thin icing. Glaze cookies when cool. Store in airtight containers.

YIELDS 7½ DOZEN 2 BY 3-INCH COOKIES.
Source: Personal notebooks of Hermilda Listeman.

Pfefferkuchen (Peppered Lebkuchen)

Cookie Dough

2 C flour	¼ t salt
1 t freshly grated nutmeg	¼ t black pepper
1 t cinnamon	¼ t cayenne pepper
1 t allspice	½ C honey
1 t ginger	½ C dark brown sugar
½ t cloves	1 egg
¼ t mace	1½ t grated lemon zest
¼ t baking soda	1½ t grated orange zest

Glaze

¼ C confectioner's sugar	½ t grated lemon zest
2 t fresh lemon juice	½ t grated orange zest
1 t fresh orange juice	

In a medium bowl, whisk together flour, spices, baking soda, salt, and peppers until thoroughly combined. In large mixing bowl, blend honey, brown sugar, egg, and lemon and orange zests. Add dry ingredients to honey mixture and stir to make a smooth, somewhat soft and sticky dough. Transfer dough onto waxed paper and shape into a flat disk ½ inch thick. Wrap and refrigerate dough overnight.

To make glaze, in a small bowl, whisk together sugar, citrus juices, and zests until smooth. Cover and set aside.

Preheat oven to 350 degrees. Lightly grease 2 large baking sheets. Working with half the dough at a time, roll dough on lightly floured surface into a large rectangle slightly less than ¼ inch thick. Cut dough into 1¼ by 2-inch rectangles. Transfer cookies to prepared baking sheets, spacing them about 1 inch apart. Bake cookies one sheet at a time for 8–10 minutes, or until edges are lightly colored and cookies are firm. Immediately transfer cookies to a rack and brush tops with reserved glaze. Let stand until the glaze sets, about 1hour. Store cookies in an airtight container for up to 3 weeks.

YIELDS ABOUT 4 DOZEN.

Aunt Annie's Papanaki

"This was Aunt Annie [Bauer]'s favorite cookie and she was the only one who really knew how to make them." The source of the name is something of a mystery.

8 C flour	2 C walnuts (ground)
pinch of salt	½ t pepper
2 C shortening	½ t cinnamon
2¼ C honey	½ t cloves
1 C sugar	½ t nutmeg
1 egg	½ t allspice

Put flour and salt in a bowl, work shortening into flour and crumble well. Add remaining ingredients and combine well. Flatten dough to about 1 inch thick and refrigerate until it can be rolled into a rectangle. If dough is dry, add egg; if thin, add more nuts. Cut dough into squares and place on cookie sheet. Bake at 375 degrees for 10 minutes.

Source: Personal notebooks of Hermilda Listeman.

Orange Tea Cookies

½ C butter
3 oz cream cheese
⅓ C honey
1 t vanilla
¼ C sugar
1 t grated orange peel

1¼ C sifted flour
1 t baking powder
½ t salt
1 C Quaker 100% Natural Cereal
2 T chocolate sprinkles

Beat butter and cream cheese together until well blended. Beat in honey and vanilla. Blend sugar with orange peel and beat into creamed mixture. Sift together flour, baking powder, and salt; stir into creamed mixture. Stir in cereal. Chill dough at least 1 hour, Shape dough into 1-inch balls. Dip each ball into chocolate sprinkles and place on ungreased cookie sheets, sprinkled side up. Bake at 350 degrees for 12–15 minutes, or until very lightly browned on edges. Remove from cookie sheets at once and cool on wire rack.

YIELDS 3½ DOZEN COOKIES.
Source: Personal notebooks of Hermilda Listeman.

Ciastka Miodowe (Polish Honey Cakes)

Popular Christmas cookies in Poland.

½ C honey
½ C sugar
2 eggs
4 C flour
1 t baking soda
½ t cinnamon

½ t nutmeg
¼ t ground cloves
¼ t ginger
1 egg yolk
50 blanched almond halves

Combine honey with sugar; beat in eggs. Sift dry ingredients together and add to honey mixture. Let dough sit overnight. Roll dough ¼ inch thick and cut with a large round cookie cutter. Brush cookie tops with beaten egg yolk and press an almond half into the center of each. Bake at 375 degrees for 15 minutes.

Hamentaschen

A traditional cookie prepared for the Jewish holiday Purim. They are shaped like the tri-cornered hat ostensibly worn by Haman, the evil minister of King Ahasuerus and villain of the Book of Esther. Some say that the name is a corruption of the German mohntaschen *(poppy seed–filled pouch); the singular of* hamentaschen *is* hamentasch. *Poppy seeds are among the more popular filling ingredients.*

1 t baking powder	½ C honey
1 t baking soda	3 eggs
½ t salt	1 T vanilla
⅔ C butter, softened	4 C flour
1 C sugar	

Filling
apricot jam, cherry preserves, *lekvar* (prune butter),
and poppy seed pie filling

Mix together all ingredients except flour. Add flour gradually until dough can be handled. Roll out dough and cut into circles approximately 3 inches in diameter. Place a tablespoon of filling in the center of each circle and fold sides up to center to form a triangle, pinching at corners to seal. Bake at 350 degrees approximately 15 minutes, or until golden brown.

YIELDS APPROXIMATELY 125 HAMENTASCHEN.
Family recipe from May Berenbaum.

Apiscotti (Bee-Enabled Biscotti)

This modification of Aunt Ruth Merkel's mandel bread recipe was submitted to the Don't Dessert Pollinators Recipe Contest sponsored by the Pollinator Partnership in 2009. Seven of the 12 ingredients (butter, honey, almond extract, nutmeg, cranberries, cherries, and almonds) depend on the pollination services of Apis mellifera, *hence the name* apiscotti. *Without* Apis mellifera, *breakfast (and every other meal) would be infinitely less interesting and colorful.*

½ C butter
½ C sugar
¼ C honey
3 eggs
½ t salt
1 t almond extract

¼ t nutmeg
2 t baking powder
2½ to 3 C flour
½ C dried cranberries, chopped
½ C dried cherries, chopped
½ C blanched sliced almonds, chopped

Preheat oven to 350 degrees. Cream butter and sugar together; mix in honey until smooth. Beat eggs until frothy and then add salt, almond extract, nutmeg, and baking powder. Combine the creamed butter with the egg mixture. Add flour until dough is a consistency that can be handled. Refrigerate dough for 1 hour or more.

Divide chilled dough into 3 parts and flatten each third into a rectangle (use additional flour to make handling easier if necessary). Place a line lengthwise down the center of each flattened section of dough and sprinkle with chopped cherries, cranberries, and nuts. Fold both sides of each rectangle in to the center over the filling, forming a loaf; seal edges. Place loaves on greased cookie sheet. Bake at 350 degrees for 45 minutes to 1 hour, or until golden brown. Cut biscotti on a slant while hot into ½-inch slices. For crispier slices, return to oven for 5–10 minutes, or until golden brown (the color of a honey bee).

Sfratti (Italian Sticks)

This pastry is popular among Sephardic Jews for Rosh Hashanah (Jewish New Year). "Sticks" refers to their shape, but sfratti *also means "evicted" and refers to a time when landlords chased away Jewish tenants during periods of intolerance. I found this recipe, handwritten and without a citation, in a notebook of vegetarian recipes I kept during graduate school.*

Pastry

3 C pastry or bleached
   all-purpose flour, sifted
1 C sugar

¼ t salt
⅓ C unsalted butter, chilled
⅔ C white wine (approximate)

Filling

1 C honey
2 t orange zest
2½ C walnuts, chopped
2 t lemon zest

¾ t ground cinnamon
¼ t each, cloves and cinnamon
⅛ t freshly ground black pepper

Glaze

1 egg beaten with 1 T water

Make a well in flour; place sugar and salt in well. Gradually cut in butter to form crumbs; sprinkle with wine, mixing with a fork until dough is smooth and stiff. Knead for 5 minutes; cover dough and refrigerate for at least 1 hour.

Make filling by bringing honey to boil in a saucepan over medium heat; simmer for 5 minutes (watch for foaming). Add remaining filling ingredients and simmer another 5 minutes, stirring constantly. Remove from heat and cool enough to handle. Pour onto a floured surface and divide into 6 portions, rolling each into a cylinder about 12 inches long.

To form sfratti, allow pastry dough to return to room temperature, then divide into 6 portions. Roll each portion into 4 by 14-inch strips. Place filling on each strip and wrap dough completely around the cylinder. Pinch the dough together along seam and at each end. Place on a floured baking sheet, seam side down. Bake 20 minutes at 375 degrees; remove from sheet, wrap each stick in foil, and cool. Right before serving, slice if desired into 2-inch sticks.

Mom's Almond Teiglach

Teiglach (or taiglach) seem to be a Rosh Hashanah (New Year's) tradition only among Lithuanian Jews. The recipe bears a strong resemblance to the Italian cicerchiata or struffoli. Whether this resemblance is coincidence, convergence, or parallel evolution is an interesting question.

Dough

2½ C sifted flour	4 eggs
½ t salt	4 T vegetable oil
1 t baking powder	

Syrup

1 C dark honey	¼ C lemon juice
¾ C brown sugar	2 C almonds, chopped
1 t ginger	½ C candied cherries (optional
½ t nutmeg	topping)
½ C water	

Sift together flour, salt, and baking powder. In a separate bowl, mix eggs and oil; make a well in the dry ingredients and pour the eggs and oil into the well. Mix together until a dough is formed. Knead the dough until it is smooth. Break off small pieces of dough and roll them by hand into pencil-thin strips. Cut each strip into ½-inch pieces and transfer to a lightly greased cookie sheet. Bake at 350 degrees for 20 minutes, or until browned. Shake pan while baking to brown on all sides. Cool.

Combine honey, brown sugar, ginger, and nutmeg in a saucepan and heat until just before boiling (approximately 15 minutes). Drop baked dough pieces a few at a time into the syrup in order to maintain temperature; cook for 5 minutes. Stir in water, lemon juice, nuts and cook for 10 more minutes, stirring frequently and shaking the pan to ensure all dough pieces are coated on all surfaces. Spread syrup and dough mixture out on a wet surface and let cool enough to handle. Form the dough-syrup-nut mixture into 3-inch balls, moistening hands whenever necessary to aid in shaping. Teiglach can be placed in cupcake liners and topped with candied cherries.

Hazelnut Teiglach

The annual fundraising project of the Sisterhood of Temple B'nai Chaim in George-town, Connecticut, is to sell the Wilton Gold honey produced by famed beekeeper Ed Weiss of Wilton, Connecticut.

4 C flour, sifted	12 oz honey
pinch of ginger	½ C sugar
1 t baking powder	8 oz chopped hazelnuts
4 eggs	pinch of powdered ginger
3 T oil	

Mix together flour, baking powder, eggs, and oil and knead until smooth. Roll dough into ropes ½ inch thick and cut the ropes into ½-inch pieces. Place honey and sugar in a saucepan and bring to a boil. Add dough pieces and continue to boil for about 5 minutes. Spoon into greased baking pan and place in oven at 375 degrees. When dough begins to puff up and turn brown, add nuts. Bake until dough pieces turn brown, stirring frequently. Take pan from oven and pour contents onto a "wet board"; allow to cool. When cool enough to handle, pat contents until flat, keeping hands moistened with cold water. Sprinkle with ginger and refrigerate.

Source: Adapted from Sharon Sobel's recipe in the Temple B'nai Chaim's *Sisterhood Cookbook,* 1996; contributed to this volume by Diane Berenbaum.

Cicerchiata, from Roberto Bruni, an Entomologist from Ascoli di Piceno, Italy

Off-hand, one of the oldest recipes in my area is the cicerchiata. According to opinion, the name *cicerchiata* comes from *cicero*, a southern expression for *cece* (garbanzo bean, chickpea, *Cicer arietinum*). In fact, the little balls of fried dough that are the basis for this dessert look a little like garbanzos.

This cake is typical of the Carnival period and has ancient origins. Traditionally a family product, it has passed to artisan production and today can be found in all pastry shops. The most typical area for the cicerchiata is, however, in the provinces of Macerata and Ascoli Piceno. It is flour mixed with eggs, a little sugar, and a drop of *mistrà,* the characteristic anis seed–flavored Marches liqueur. The mixture is rolled into small balls that are then fried in oil or lard, mixed with honey, and put together to shape a flat ring that may then be sprinkled with pine nuts. The cake can be shaped in various ways (e.g., a rounded pyramid) by sticking the dough balls together with honey.

The origin of this cake should be considered ancient Umbria (now Umbria and Marche), particularly in the Piceno Territory, which in the past included part of the Abruzzo. A very similar cake was cited in the eighteenth-century *"tavole eugubine"* (Gubbio tablets) as a ritual and sacrificial. It was called *strusia*, from *sruikela*, a diminutive for *struex* (a pile of something), according to Augusto Ancilotti, a specialist in the old Umbrian language. From the same root comes the Italian verb *costruire* (to build, put together). This is very near to the Neapolitan's struffoli from the Greek adjective *stróngylos* (round shape) and by linguistic point of view sharing the same root of the Umbrian word *strusia* and therefore (probably) a common proto-Indo-European linguistic origin.

It is remarkable that today in Greece there is a cake called *lukumádes*. Quite probably, the name cicerchiata has a medieval origin and should come from *cicerchia* (*Lathyrus sativus*), a legume very similar to pea (*Pisum sativum*) or to *cece* and common in the Umbrian area at that time. In the end, the meaning of the word *cicerchiata* should be "a pile of cicerchie."

Struffoli, one of Carnival's most spectacular specialties, are also very typical of the Campania Region and prepared with dozens of balls of fried batter that are then rolled in honey and decorated with colored sugar strands known as *cannulli* or *diavolulli*. The name of this sweet derives from the Greek *strongulos* (a rounded body), which refers to the shape of the batter before it is fried. In Central Italy a similar sweet, cicerchiata, is prepared. The abundant use of candied fruit, almonds, sugared almonds, and honey reveal the ancient roots of the recipe.

Struffoli (Italian Honey Balls)

2½ C flour
1 T baking powder
5 eggs, beaten
¼ C shortening
½ T sugar
dash of salt

½ t lemon zest or 1 t orange zest
2 C vegetable oil for frying
1½ C honey (orange blossom
   works well)
1 t orange zest
colored sprinkles for decoration
   (optional)

Sift together flour and baking powder. Place flour on board, making a well in the center. Place eggs, shortening, sugar, salt, and lemon or orange zest into the well. Mix well, working the dough by hand. Shape into very small balls, the size of marbles. Let the dough balls rest 15–20 minutes, covered with damp paper towels, while heating the oil to 350 degrees in a deep pot. Drop the balls, a few at a time, into the hot oil until golden brown. They'll float, so turn them for even browning. Melt honey in a saucepan and add orange zest. As soon as the balls are fried, place them directly from the oil into the honey; allow them to float for about 30 seconds. Lift balls from honey with a slotted spoon, and place on a serving platter in the shape of a cone. Decorate with colored sprinkles while the honey is still warm.

Mostaccioli (Mustache) Cookies

1 C hazelnuts
1 C walnuts
⅓ C honey
1 egg white
1 T unsweetened cocoa powder

½ t cinnamon
⅛ t ground cloves
pinch of salt
⅓ C flour
powdered sugar

Icing
½ C powdered sugar, sifted
1 T egg white, beaten to blend

1–2 t orange liqueur

Preheat oven to 275 degrees. Finely grind nuts in a food processor. Add honey, egg white, cocoa, spices, and salt and blend to a paste. Add flour and mix by pulsing until just incorporated (dough will be sticky). Place dough on work surface heavily dusted with sifted powdered sugar. Sift more sugar over the dough. Gently roll dough out to ⅜ inch thick. Cut into 1 by 1½-inch bars using a knife dusted with powdered sugar. Arrange on greased baking sheet, spacing 1 inch apart. Bake cookies until firm and tops appear dry, about 25–30 minutes. Cool cookies completely on racks.

To make icing, combine powdered sugar and egg white and beat until blended; add enough liqueur so icing is still thick but pourable. Set racks over waxed paper; arrange cooled cookies on racks with edges touching. Drizzle icing over cookies in irregular lines. Separate cookies. Let stand until icing is dry. Store in airtight container

Source: Personal notebooks of Hermilda Listeman.

Hungarian Walnut Horseshoes

Reed Johnson, an entomologist who studies honey bees, discovered this recipe. "When I was teaching English to private students in Hungary," he writes, "I was making about $2 an hour. But many students' grandmothers felt the need to pay me a bonus in the form of some sort of Hungarian baked goods to take home with me. There were little apple pies and poppy seed rolls and chestnut delicacies, but one of my favorites was the honey-filled walnut horseshoe. While it is traditionally a Christmas treat in Hungary I think it is good any time of the year."

Dough

⅓ C warm milk	1½ C flour
¼ t yeast	¼ t salt
1½ t sugar	1 T sour cream
½ C butter	

Filling

¼ C milk	2 C walnuts, chopped
¾ C honey	breadcrumbs (if needed to
1 t vanilla	thicken mixture)

Glaze

1 egg yolk, beaten

To make the dough, combine warm milk, yeast, and sugar in a small bowl and let proof for 10–15 minutes. In a large bowl incorporate butter into flour and salt with a pastry blender or 2 knives until the butter is in pea-sized pieces. Make a well in the flour mixture and add the yeast mixture and the sour cream. Mix to combine and knead briefly on a floured board until smooth.

To make the filling, bring the milk to a boil in a small saucepan. Remove the pan from heat and add honey, vanilla, and walnuts to the milk. Combine to make a spreadable mixture; add breadcrumbs to thicken if needed.

Roll out the dough on a floured board in a large rectangle. Spread the filling evenly on the dough and roll it, starting from one of the longer sides. Tuck in the edges as you go. Place the roll on an ungreased cookie sheet in the shape of a horseshoe. Brush the top with egg yolk and allow a few minutes to dry. Poke holes in the horseshoe with a skewer or fork and bake at 350 degrees for 30–40 minutes until brown.

Almond Won Ton Cookies

Hilda Ganadot, married to a diplomat, lived in Asia for five years and gave this recipe to Hermilda, who noted, "Delicious. Crispy. Very special. Unusual wonderful filling."

¾ C almonds,
   toasted and finely chopped
⅓ C flaked coconut
⅓ C honey
1 t cinnamon

½ lb fresh won ton wrappers
   (fresh, not frozen)
4 C vegetable oil for deep-frying
confectioner's sugar

Note: To toast almonds in a microwave, place 1 T butter in 9-inch pie plate. Microwave on high for 30–45 seconds, or until butter is melted. Stir in ¾ C almonds. Microwave 3–4 minutes, stirring every 2 minutes. Let stand for 5 minutes. Chop almonds fine so they will not pierce the skins.

Combine almonds, coconut, honey, and cinnamon in a small mixing bowl; mix until well blended. Place 1 t almond mixture in center of each won ton wrapper.

Moisten edges of wrapper with water, fold in half to form a triangle, and seal the edges carefully, then bring opposite points together, pinching edges to seal. (Fresh won ton wrappers are easier to fold and fry, seal better, and leak less.) Shape all the cookies before frying. Keep the wrappers and shaped cookies covered to prevent drying out.

Heat oil to 375 degrees in a wok (or deep skillet), and deep-fry the won tons a few at a time for about 2 minutes each. Remove from oil and drain and cool on paper towels. Dust with confectioner's sugar. Best if consumed right away but can be stored in an airtight container for a few days.

YIELDS 3 DOZEN COOKIES.

Korean Honey Flour Cakes

There are about 2 million beehives in Korea, and they produce about 1,000 tons of honey annually. Domestic production doesn't meet demand, so Koreans import large quantities of honey from overseas; clover honey from the United States is among the most popular. "Cliff honey" made by the rock bee, *Apis dorsata,* from Nepal is also imported for its putative medicinal properties.

1¼ C honey	2 C flour
¼ C white wine	2 T sesame oil
1¼ C water	4 C vegetable oil for frying

In a small saucepan, combine ¼ C honey, wine, and ¼ C water; cook over low heat for 5 minutes, stirring continuously. Allow to cool. Combine honey mixture with flour and oil and knead dough for 3 minutes. Roll the dough to a thickness of ¼ inch and cut out flower shapes with cookie cutters. In a separate pot, combine the remaining 1 C honey and 1 C water and heat gently for 5 minutes. Allow to cool. Heat cooking oil in frying pan and deep-fry the flower cookies until they float to the top of the oil; immediately remove the cookies, transfer them to honey water, and allow them to soak for 24–48 hours.

YIELDS APPROXIMATELY 24 COOKIES.

Bourma (Nut Roll)

2 C walnuts, grated
   or finely chopped
⅓ C sugar
pinch of cinnamon (optional)

pinch of ground cloves (optional)
1 lb phyllo sheets
1½ C clarified butter, melted

Syrup

1½ C water
2 t lemon juice
½ C honey

cinnamon stick (optional)
1½ C sugar

Mix together walnuts, sugar, cinnamon, and cloves. Spread a single phyllo sheet on a flat surface; keep remaining sheets covered to prevent drying. Brush phyllo sheet with melted butter. Sprinkle teaspoonful of walnut-spice mixture across the middle part of the sheet, then fold it away from you to make an even line. Roll dough loosely around a wooden dowel about ¼ inch in diameter, lightly brush with melted butter, and finish rolling the sheet to its end. Brush outside seam with butter. After the entire sheet is rolled, use the thumb and forefinger of each hand to gently push each end toward the center to crimp. Slide the dowel out and place the roll of phyllo onto a 17 by 14-inch buttered baking sheet. Repeat until all phyllo sheets have been used.

Arrange bourmas side by side on a baking sheet and brush each with melted butter. Bake at 375 degrees for approximately 20–25 minutes, or until light golden. Remove from oven, cool on paper towels. To make syrup, combine ingredients in a small saucepan. Bring to a boil and cook, stirring occasionally, for 10 minutes. Remove cinnamon stick and cool. Cut each bourma into 2–3 pieces and pour cooled syrup over them before serving.

Honey Almond Cookies

2 C flour
½ t baking soda
⅛ t salt
¼ C butter, softened
⅓ C sugar
⅓ C honey
1 T vegetable oil

1½ t vanilla
1 t almond extract
1½ T grated orange peel
1 egg white
2–3 T butter, melted
¼ C sliced almonds, chopped

Combine flour, baking soda, and salt in a bowl. Cream butter, sugar, honey, and oil in a separate bowl; add extracts, orange peel, and egg white and beat until well blended. Stir in flour mixture (dough will be sticky). Coat hands lightly with cooking spray and divide dough into 2 equal portions. Shape each portion into a 9-inch log. Wrap logs individually in plastic wrap. Freeze 3 hours, or until firm.

Preheat oven to 375 degrees. Cut each log into 24 ¼-inch slices and place 1 inch apart on greased baking sheets. Brush tops of cookies with melted butter, press almonds into cookies. Bake at 375 degrees for 9 minutes. Cool a few minutes, or until firm. Remove cookies from pans; cool on wire racks.

YIELDS 4 DOZEN COOKIES.

Chapter 6

Breads, Quick Breads, and Muffins

Grandma Berenbaum's Challah

My grandmother, Ida Berenbaum, made this challah from memory. This version was recorded as my cousin, Lisa Strauch, shadowed Grandmother and measured everything as it went into the bowl.

2 pkg yeast
2½ C warm water
4 eggs, beaten
⅔ C vegetable oil

5–6 T honey
4 t salt
10–15 C flour
3 yolks, beaten (for glaze)

Dissolve yeast in warm water. Add eggs, oil, honey, salt, and 6 C flour. Beat thoroughly with wooden spoon. Gradually add more flour until the dough is too stiff to bend. Place remaining flour on pastry board; knead until dough is smooth and flour is absorbed. If it's still sticky, add more flour. Place dough in a large covered bowl. Let it rise in a warm place for 1½ hours, or until tripled in bulk. Punch down and divide into 16 portions. Shape each portion into a rope 1 inch in diameter. Use 4 ropes to braid each loaf. Place each loaf in a pan and allow to rise for 45 minutes, or until almost tripled in bulk. Brush top with egg wash. Bake at 375 degrees for 25–30 minutes, or until golden brown.

YIELDS 4 SMALL LOAVES.

Oatmeal Honey Bread

This recipe from Lee Solter, an insect pathologist at the Illinois Natural History Survey, and her husband, Phil, was modified from a Dell Publishing minibook on breads. Lee says this bread has a very slight edge of sweetness, making it perfect for hot buttered breakfast toast but not too sweet for sandwiches.

2 C boiling water	½ C lukewarm water
1 C rolled oats (not quick oats)	2 t salt
1 T butter	½ C honey
1 package yeast (or 1 T)	4½-5 C unbleached white flour

Pour boiling water over oats and butter in a medium bowl; stir and let stand until lukewarm. Mix yeast with lukewarm water in a large bowl and allow to bloom. Add cooled oatmeal to yeast and stir; add salt, honey, and 2 C flour. Mix well. Slowly mix in remaining flour until dough is firm and easy to handle. Knead bread by hand for 8 minutes, or 4 minutes with a dough hook on a standing mixer. Place dough in a greased bowl, cover, and let rise until doubled in bulk, 1–2 hours. Punch down, divide into 2 sections, and let stand 5 minutes. Shape into 2 loaves and place in greased bread pans. Cover with towel or oiled plastic wrap for a second rising, 45–60 minutes. Bake at 350 degrees for 40–50 minutes until top is brown.

Unleavened Carob Bread

Carob is sometimes known as St. John's bread because the seed pods are believed to be the "locusts" John fed upon in Matthew 3:4: "Now John wore a garment of camel's hair and a leather girdle around his waist; and his food was locusts and wild honey."

2⅔ C water	1 C rolled oats (not quick oats)
5 T white bread flour	3 T carob
¼ C honey	¾ C chopped dates or figs
⅗ C sesame seeds, toasted	1 T oil
5½ C whole wheat flour	1 t salt

Mix all ingredients together. Knead well for a soft pliable dough. Place in oiled bowl and cover with towel; let sit overnight. The next morning, shape into 2 round loaves and let them sit for an hour in a warm spot. The bread may or may not rise at this point—the softer and more pliable the dough, the better the chance it will rise. Before baking, cut an X lightly on top to prevent cracking. Bake at 350 degrees for 50–60 minutes until browned and hollow-sounding when tapped.

YIELDS 2 ROUND LOAVES.

Honey-Glazed Bran Muffins

1 C bran	⅓ C butter
1 C buttermilk	½ C brown sugar
1 C flour	1 egg
1 t cinnamon	¼ C molasses
1 t baking powder	⅓ C raisins
½ t baking soda	⅓ C chopped dates
½ t salt	

Glaze

¾ C honey	1 T butter
⅓ C corn syrup	

Preheat oven to 400 degrees. Line muffin pan with 12 paper cups.

Combine bran and buttermilk. Mix together flour, cinnamon, baking powder, baking soda, and salt. Add all at once to bran mixture, stirring just to mix. Cream together butter, brown sugar, egg, and molasses. Blend into bran mixture. Stir in raisins and dates. Fill muffin cups ¾ full. Bake 20–25 minutes. Cool slightly; remove papers.

In saucepan, combine honey, corn syrup, and butter. Bring to boil over medium heat. Reduce heat and simmer 5 minutes. Place muffins, one at a time, in glaze, using a spoon to coat each one thoroughly. Place on cookie sheet until glaze is set. Serve warm with butter.

Source: Personal notebooks of Hermilda Listeman.

Pain d'épices facile

"This recipe," observes Claudine Fréard Rose, a teacher of French and a friend of the Department of Entomology at the University of Illinois at Urbana-Champaign, "is one I have made before; it is a very simple variation of pain d'épices. Now this is a basic easy French recipe." Traditionally, pain d'épices, which dates back to the reign of Charles VII (1429–61), was made with a "mother dough" (pâte-mère) made by combining honey and rye flour and allowing the mixture to sit and ripen for days or months. Honey, with its antimicrobial properties, prevented spoilage. No one, of course, has time for such preparations now, hence this version. Dark buckwheat honey is the one of choice for preparing this specialty.

8 oz honey (strong fragrant varieties preferred)	¼ C brown sugar
½ C hot milk	1 egg
7 T unsalted butter, melted	pinch of salt
1½ C flour	2 t mixed spices (cinnamon, ground ginger, ground cloves, ground nutmeg)
1 t, heaping, baking powder	

Preheat oven to 350 degrees. In a bowl, add honey to the hot milk; stir well until the honey is well-dissolved. Add melted butter to the bowl and then the flour. Stir well so the mixture is smooth. Stir in the baking powder, brown sugar, egg, pinch of salt, and spices. Butter a loaf pan or line it with parchment paper, which makes cleaning up much easier and the bread is sure not to stick to the pan. Pour in the batter and bake in the preheated oven for 35 minutes.

Honey Spice Cake (Pain d'épices)

Most people agree that honey spice cake tastes better after it has aged a bit, and some will even wait several days before eating it. Wrap the cake in plastic wrap and save it at room temperature or in the refrigerator. It also freezes very well.

¾ C milk	½ t ginger
¾ C honey	¼ t allspice

6 T butter	¼ t ground cloves
3 C flour	1 egg, lightly beaten
2 T sugar	⅓ C chopped candied ginger
2 t baking powder	(optional)
1 t cinnamon	1 t anise seeds (optional)

Heat the milk in a small saucepan on low heat until warm to the touch. Add the honey and stir until blended. Stir in the butter until it is completely melted. Remove from the heat and cool until just warm.

In a large mixing bowl, sift the flour with the sugar, baking powder, and spices. Stir in the cooled milk mixture and egg; mix until well blended. Mix in the candied ginger and anise seeds if you are using them. The dough will be stiff and sticky.

Butter and flour an 8-cup loaf pan. Spread dough in the pan, pushing it to fill the corners. Bake at 350 degrees for 50 minutes. Cool cake thoroughly and cover in plastic wrap to store.

Buckweat Honey Muffins

2 C all-purpose flour	¼ t salt
2 T wheat germ	1 egg
¼ C sugar	1 C milk
¼ C brown sugar	¼ C butter, melted
3 t baking powder	¼ C buckwheat honey

Preheat oven to 400 degrees. Line muffin pan with paper cups. In a large bowl, sift together flour, wheat germ, sugars, baking powder, and salt. In a separate bowl, beat together egg and milk. Add butter and honey to egg-milk mixture. Add the liquid mixture into dry ingredients and stir just until blended; do not over-mix. Fill muffin cups ⅔ full, and bake for 15 minutes until the muffins are a light, golden brown.

Honey Muffins

Much honey in Illinois comes from nectar produced by soybeans. Soy honey is a double boon for the state. It is flavorful and rich in antioxidants, and bee visitation increases pod filling and crop yields even though soybeans can self-pollinate. This recipe comes from 1929, before soybeans were planted extensively in the state and when the most important nectar sources for Illinois bees were white, alsike, and sweet clover, and, particularly in southern Illinois, heartsease and Spanish needle.

1 egg, beaten lightly	½ t salt
2 T honey	4 t baking powder
2 T shortening	1½ C milk
2 C white flour	

Mix beaten eggs with shortening and honey. Sift together flour, salt, and baking powder. To the egg mixture, alternately add milk and dry ingredients. Beat until mixture is smooth and creamy. Pour into well-greased muffin tins and bake at 400 degrees for 20–25 minutes. Serve with honey.

Variations: Many different kinds of muffins may be developed using the basic muffin batter and adding, before baking, such fruits or nuts as the following to each muffin cup after it is filled with batter: 2 salted pecans, 4 to 6 peanuts, walnuts, pieces of cooked prunes, pieces of apricot, 2 cherries, diced pineapple, strawberries, and other variations.

Source: Adapted from Vern Milum, University of Illinois Extension Service mimeographed bulletin, 1929.

Honey Oatmeal Gems

This recipe won first prize in the Honey Oatmeal Cookie Division at the Illinois State Fair in 1934.

½ C shortening	2 T baking soda
1 C honey	2 T baking powder
½ C sugar	3 C rolled oats (not quick oats)
1¼ C milk	1 C seedless raisins
1 T vanilla	1 C nuts, chopped
3 C flour	

Cream shortening, honey, and sugar thoroughly; then add milk and vanilla; mix well. Sift flour with baking powder and soda and add to creamed mixture. Stir in oats, raisins, and nuts. Pour in greased muffin tins and bake at 400 degrees for 20 minutes.

Source: Adapted from the *Annual Report of the Illinois State Beekeepers Association,* 1934.

First-Prize Honey Gingerbread

This is the first-prize recipe from the honey gingerbread category of the Honey Culinary Competition at the 1934 State Fair.

1 C butter	3 C flour
½ C sugar	2 t baking soda
½ C honey	1 t cinnamon
1 C molasses	1 t cloves
3 eggs, beaten	2 t ginger
1 C buttermilk (or sour cream)	pinch of salt

Cream sugar, honey, molasses, and butter. Add eggs, and milk, and mix well. Sift together dry ingredients and add to creamed liquid ingredients, mixing until well blended. Pour into a greased and floured 9 by 9-inch pan. Bake at 350 degrees for 30 minutes, or until center tests done.

French Gingerbread

6 C flour
2 C rice flour
2½ T baking powder
2 C honey
2 C butter

zest of 2 lemons, minced
1 C almond paste
2 T ground ginger
½ t ground nutmeg
pinch ground cloves

Combine flour, rice flour, and baking powder and sift 6 times. Put honey and butter in warm jar and keep warm until butter is melted. Mince the zest of 2 lemons and mix with almond paste and spices. Stir the honey and spice mixtures into the flour and beat hard for 20 minutes. Bake in 2 or 3 buttered pans in a moderate oven (350 degrees). Cover with light icing and cut when cool.

Source: Adapted from *The All-American Cook Book,* 1922, page 162, in the Community Cookbook Collection of Hermilda Listeman (University of Illinois Library).

Pão de mel (Brazilian Honey-Spice Bread)

This bread is traditionally baked not as a loaf but more like a biscuit or cookie and dipped in melted chocolate after baking. A less labor-intensive alternative is to bake it in a 9 by 13-inch pan and add grated chocolate when it comes out of the oven.

⅓ C milk
⅔ C brown sugar
2 C flour
1½ t baking powder
½ t cinnamon

¼ t nutmeg
¼ t cloves
½ C honey
2 eggs, beaten
⅓ C vegetable oil

Glaze

½ C bittersweet
chocolate, grated
⅓ C heavy cream

¼ C corn syrup
1 t vanilla extract

In a saucepan, mix milk and sugar; stir over low heat until the sugar dissolves. In a bowl, combine dry ingredients. Stir in milk mixture, then add honey, eggs, and oil. Pour batter into a greased 8-inch loaf pan. Bake at 350 degrees for 55–60 minutes. Cool in pan.

Prepare glaze in a saucepan, combining chocolate, cream, corn syrup, and vanilla; heat until mixture boils and then remove from heat. Pour glaze over the cooled loaf.

Yemarina Yewotet Dabo (Spiced Ethiopian Honey Bread)

A popular item for breaking the Ramadan fast among Muslim Ethiopians.

¼ C lukewarm water	4–5 C flour
½ C honey	1 T ground coriander
1 package active dried yeast	½ t cloves
6 T butter, melted	1 t salt
1 egg, beaten	1 C lukewarm milk

Glaze

1 egg, beaten	4 T milk

In a small bowl, stir together water and honey; sprinkle in yeast and allow to sit until frothy, about 10 minutes. Add butter and eggs to yeast mixture. In a separate bowl, sift flour with coriander, cloves, and salt. Stir in yeast mixture and add milk, stirring until a firm dough forms. Place dough on a floured surface and knead until dough is smooth and stretches, about 20 minutes. Place dough in a lightly greased bowl, cover with a damp towel, and allow to rise until double in size, at least 1½ hours. Knead the dough again and divide into 3 portions; roll each portion into a sausage shape and braid to form a loaf. Move the loaf to a well-greased baking sheet, cover with a damp towel, and allow to rise in a warm place until double in size, approximately 1 hour. To make glaze, combine beaten egg with milk. Brush the top of the loaf with the glaze. Bake at 350 degrees for about 30 minutes, or until golden.

Beehive Bread

Beehive bread is good with honey butter.

6 C all-purpose flour	½ C honey
⅔ C whole wheat flour	2 T brown sugar
1½ t salt	½ C butter or margarine
2 envelopes quick-acting yeast	2 eggs
1¼ C water	

Glaze

1 egg, beaten	1 T water

Mix together 2 C flour, salt, and undissolved yeast. In a saucepan, heat water, honey, sugar, and butter until very warm. Gradually beat liquid mixture into dry ingredients, using an electric mixer at medium speed, scraping bowl continuously, for about 2 minutes. Add eggs and another cup of flour; beat for another 2 minutes. Add remaining flour and stir until soft dough forms. Knead on floured surface until smooth and stretchy (about 10 minutes). Cover and let sit for 10 minutes.

Divide dough into 20 equal-sized pieces. Make a 20-inch rope from each piece. Twist 2 ropes together and press ends together; repeat with remaining 18 ropes. Upend a 2½-quart ovenproof mixing bowl onto a greased baking sheet; spray sides of bowl with nonstick cooking spray. Wrap the rope twists around the bowl, starting at the bottom rim and pinching the ends to connect the twists. Wrap until the entire bowl is covered. Cover with a damp towel and allow to rise in warm place until puffy (approximately ½ hour).

To make the glaze, beat together egg and water; brush over dough. Bake at 375 degrees for 25–30 minutes. Remove from oven and cool on bowl for 15 minutes. Make a foil ball approximately the same dimensions as the inside of the bowl and place it on a wire rack; remove the "breadhive" from the bowl carefully and place it over the ball to finish cooling.

Bint al-Sahn (Yemeni Honey Bread)

No international honey cookbook would be complete without a recipe from Yemen, which has a long tradition of beekeeping. In a fifteenth-century Arabic text on the topic by al-Magrizi, Yemen is identified as "a land of honey." The nation now produces 1,800 tons annually from such floral sources as apricots, almonds, and Christ's thorn. Yemeni honey made the news in October 2001 when two men were arrested in New York en route to Yemen with boxes of honey that concealed $140,000 in cash. The terrorist network Al Qaeda has a history of using honey as the basis for smuggling. Retail honey shops generate income, and drugs and weapons are concealed in shipments of honey.

1 package yeast	4 C flour
½ C warm water	½ t salt
5 eggs, beaten	1¼ C butter, melted
2 T milk	1 C honey

Dissolve yeast in warm water. Mix yeast with eggs and milk. In a separate bowl, mix together flour and salt and form a well in the middle. Pour the yeast mixture into the well and stir into a dough; knead dough, adding ¼ C melted butter. Knead until a smooth elastic dough results (you may add more flour or milk if necessary). Cover and allow to rest in a warm place for 1 hour. Divide the dough into 12 balls and place on a floured surface; cover with a damp towel and allow them to rest for another half hour. Roll each ball of dough into an 8-inch round. Place 1 round into a buttered pie pan and brush with melted butter. Add 5 more rounds, buttering each, and pressing edges to attach rounds. In a second buttered pie pan, repeat with the remaining 6 rounds. Mix the remaining butter with honey and brush the top of each stack with some of the honey-butter mixture. Bake at 350 degrees for 25 minutes, or until the top round is golden. Remove from oven and pour remaining butter-honey mixture over both pans. Allow to rest for 20 minutes and then slice into wedges.

Sweet Potato Honey Bread

A modification of a family recipe.

½ C vegetable oil
1 C honey
3 eggs
1½ C sweet potato (pureed
    or canned)
1 t vanilla
2 C flour

½ C sugar
1½ t baking soda
¼ t salt
1 t cinnamon
½ t nutmeg
½ C water or milk
½ C raisins or pecans (optional)

Measure oil and pour into bowl; measure honey in the same cup and add to bowl (this makes the honey easier to pour out of the cup). Blend honey and oil; mix in eggs, sweet potato, and vanilla until smooth. In a separate bowl, mix together all dry ingredients. Fold dry ingredients into the sweet potato mixture, alternating with water (or milk). Raisins or pecans can be added at this stage if tossed with flour. Pour batter into 2 greased and floured 9 by 5-inch loaf pans. Bake at 375 degrees for about 1 hour, or until bread tests done. Cool in pan 10–15 minutes and then remove.

Chapter 7

No-Bake, Boiled, and Fried Desserts

Grandma Jesse's Imberlach

This recipe is one variation of a honey candy served on Rosh Hashanah. "Imber" is derived from the German word for ginger, "ingwer."

2 C matzo farfel	½ C sugar
1 egg, beaten	2 t ground ginger
¼ C orange juice	1 t ground cinnamon
1 C honey	1 C walnuts (or hazelnuts), chopped

Place farfel in a bowl; mix in beaten egg. Place on a baking sheet in an oven on low heat for 10 minutes. In a large saucepan, bring orange juice, honey, sugar, ginger and cinnamon to a boil over moderate heat. Stir until sugar dissolves, then mix in farfel and nuts. Boil mixture for 10 minutes, stirring occasionally. Moisten a wooden board with cold water; pour out honey-farfel mix and flatten with a wooden spoon. Allow to cool and then cut into diamonds.

No-Bake Orange Ginger Cookie Balls

Make these cookies the day before or up to 2 weeks ahead.

1/2 lb. gingersnaps (about 40)	1 T orange zest
1½ C pecans, chopped	3 T honey
¼ C orange juice	

Finely grind gingersnaps and ¾ C pecans in a food processor. Add orange juice and zest and honey and mix well. Shape gingersnap mixture by hand into 1-inch balls and roll in remaining chopped pecans to coat. Store cookies in tightly covered container to mellow flavors for at least a day.

YIELDS ABOUT 2½ DOZEN.

Parisian Sweets

2½ C dates
2½ C dried figs
2½ C nuts of choice
2 T orange juice

¼ C honey
chopped nuts, flaked coconut,
    shaved chocolate (as desired)

Put fruits and nuts through meat grinder and mix thoroughly. Add orange juice and honey. Shape into balls and roll in your choices of nuts, coconut, or shaved chocolate.

Source: Adapted from Marjorie Beebe, *The College Woman's Cook Book,* 1923, page 87, in the Community Cookbook Collection of Hermilda Listeman (University of Illinois Library).

Honey Drops

1 C powdered milk
1 C graham cracker crumbs
1 C honey

1 C raisins
1 C peanut butter
melted chocolate or flaked
    coconut (optional)

Mix powdered milk and graham cracker crumbs; stir in honey. Mix in raisins and peanut butter. Form into balls. Balls can be dipped in melted chocolate and/or rolled in coconut.

Source: American Honey Queen recipe brochure, 1983, published by the American Beekeeping Federation.

Uncooked Fruitcake

1 C grape juice	1½ C dried currants
1 C thickened blackberry juice	2½ C dates
1 cinnamon stick	1½ C dried figs
3–4 whole cloves	1½ C candied cherries
¼ t allspice	1½ C crystallized pineapple
⅛ t nutmeg	¾ C citron
2 C rolled oats (not quick oats)	1¾ C shelled pecans
1½ C wheat biscuit	¾ C flavorful honey
1½ C seeded raisins	4 T olive oil

In a saucepan, combine the fruit juices with cinnamon, cloves, allspice, and nutmeg. Bring to a simmer over low heat (do not let the juice boil rapidly). Simmer until juice is well flavored with the spices, then remove from heat and strain juice through cheesecloth.

Run the oatmeal and wheat biscuit through a food grinder before measuring. Reheat the fruit juice to boiling and pour over the cereals; cover mixture closely and set aside overnight.

Prepare the fruit and the nuts. The raisins, dates, figs, pineapple, and citron should be cut into bits, and the cherries left whole; the nuts are best broken into small pieces. When ready to prepare batter, measure the honey and olive oil into a large bowl and add the oatmeal and fruit juice mixture. Add the fruit and nuts and work by hand into mixture. Blend everything thoroughly.

Line a baking pan with baking paper brushed with olive oil. Pack the fruit mixture in the pan, a little at a time, pressing it down until it is perfectly solid. Decorate the top with nuts and cherries and cover batter with baking paper brushed with oil.

Put the cake in a covered bread tin in a cool place for several weeks or longer. Several days before cutting, wrap the fruitcake in a cloth that has been moistened with grape juice.

Source: Adapted from *The All-American Cook Book,* 1922, page 132, in the Community Cookbook Collection of Hermilda Listeman (University of Illinois Library).

No-Bake Bumblebee Cookies

This recipe not only makes use of bee products but it also makes bees—the dough can be molded into bee shapes and decorated with stripes. It is suitable for all ages; one group of college freshmen in a seminar loved making them.

1 C peanut butter	5 T crushed cereal
3 T honey	sliced almonds
⅔ C powdered skim milk	ready-made chocolate decorator icing
4 T sesame seeds	

Mix together peanut butter and honey; add powdered milk, sesame seeds, and crushed cereal. Dough should be easy to handle. By tablespoons, mold into the shape of a bee; insert 4 sliced almonds for wings (2 on each side) and use the icing to add stripes. Refrigerate for approximately a half hour.

Refrigerator Apple Honey Pie

1 9-inch cookie crust

Filling

1½ C apple juice	pinch of salt
1 pkg gelatin	1½ C chopped apple
¼ C honey	1 T lemon juice
1 t apple pie spice mix	½ C chopped walnuts

Honey Cream

2 egg whites	¾ C honey

In a small dish, combine ½ C apple juice and gelatin; place the dish in a shallow pan filled halfway with boiling water and stir the mixture until the gelatin dissolves. Then stir in the remainder of the apple juice and the honey, spice mix, and salt. Allow to cool and then refrigerate until thick and syrupy. Sprinkle the chopped apples with lemon juice and then stir the apples into the gelatin mixture; fold in nuts. Pour filling into cookie crust and chill thoroughly.

To make topping, beat cream until soft peaks form; dribble in honey, beating until stiff peaks form. Top pie with honey cream before serving.

Sweet Apple Pancakes

1 C whole-wheat flour	1 T honey
1 C all-purpose flour	1 T molasses
2 t baking soda	1 T butter, melted
2 t baking powder	2 t lemon juice
1 t cinnamon	2 eggs, beaten
½ t salt	2 C chopped Granny Smith apples
dash of nutmeg	cooking spray
2 C low-fat buttermilk	

In a large bowl, combine dry ingredients and stir well. In a small bowl, combine buttermilk, honey, molasses, butter, lemon juice, and eggs and stir well. Add buttermilk mixture to flour, stirring until smooth. Fold in apple. Let stand 5 minutes. For each pancake, spoon about ¼ C batter onto a hot, nonstick griddle or nonstick skillet coated with cooking spray. Turn pancakes when tops are covered with bubbles and edges appear to be cooked.

YIELDS 14 PANCAKES.

Apple Pancakes with Honey

1¼ C flour	1 egg
2 t baking powder	¾ C apple cider
½ t apple pie spice	⅓ C milk
¼ t salt	2 T honey
⅛ t baking soda	1 T cooking oil

Combine flour, baking powder, apple pie spice, salt, and baking soda. Beat together egg, apple juice, milk, honey, and oil. Add liquid ingredients all at once to flour mixture, stirring just until combined but still lumpy. Heat a lightly greased skillet or griddle on medium heat. Pour about ¼ C batter for each pancake onto hot skillet. Cook for 1–2 minutes, or until pancakes have a bubbly surface and slightly dry edges. Turn and cook for 1–2 minutes more, or until golden brown.

YIELDS 10 PANCAKES.

Persian Pistachio Nougat

2 eggs, separated	¼ C water
2 C granulated sugar	¼ t salt
½ C honey	1½ t rose water
1 C light corn syrup	1 C toasted pistachios

Beat egg whites until stiff. In saucepan, combine sugar, honey, corn syrup, water, and salt and cook over medium heat until sugar dissolves. Keep cooking until mixture reaches 250 degrees (forms a hard ball). Remove from heat and slowly add approximately ¼ of the mixture into the egg whites, beating constantly.

Cook remainder of sugar syrup over medium-high heat until the mixture hardens and cracks (300 degrees). While continuously stirring, slowly stir syrup into egg white mixture and stir until mixture is thick. Add rose water, fold in nuts, and stir until blended.

Oil the bottom and sides of a baking pan. Spoon the nougat into the prepared pan and press it smoothly and evenly. Refrigerate until firm. Unmold and cut into squares.

Source: Saber Miresmalli, a postdoctoral student in entomology at the University of Illinois at Urbana-Champaign.

Zoolbia

According to Saber Miresmalli, zoolbia is the "most favorite sweet" in Iran during the month of Ramadan when Muslims fast and is usually eaten with black tea in the evenings when fasts are broken.

2 C cornstarch	¾ C yogurt (not skim)
¼ C sugar	2 C cooking oil
2 T rose water	

Syrup

1 C sugar	1 T honey
3 T rose water	1 C water

Mix cornstarch, sugar, rose water, and yogurt until smooth. Heat oil in a frying pan. Using a funnel, pour the batter into the hot oil, creating round lattice shapes about 5–6 inches in diameter. Reduce heat and fry fully on one side, then on the other. For syrup, mix sugar, rose water, honey, and water. Heat until mixture boils and then thickens. Remove from heat. Soak zoolbia in the syrup for about 5 minutes and serve.

SERVES 4.

Ranginak

Saber Miresmailli says that ranginak is a traditional Persian date cake from the Province of Fars and the city of Shiraz. "It is not just the wine that is famous," he maintains, "but ranginak also has a great reputation. It has long been known as the Persian version of Viagra. And apparently it works."

1 C vegetable oil	3 C pitted dates
1½ C wheat flour	1 C walnuts
½ C powdered sugar	1 T honey
1 t cinnamon	1 T ground pistachio
½ t cardamom	

Heat oil in a pan until hot. Stir in wheat flour and turn down the heat slightly. Stir frequently until flour turns golden. Remove from heat and cool slightly. Add sugar, cinnamon, and cardamom to flour and mix well. Pour ½ the flour mixture into a flat dish and smooth with the back of a spoon. Insert a piece of walnut inside each date and place the dates on the flour mixture. Cover the dates with the rest of the flour mixture that has been mixed with honey. Flatten the mixture with the back of a spoon. Sprinkle ground pistachios on top. Cut into diamond-shaped pieces and serve.

SERVES 4.

Cornmeal Hoecakes

According to his step-granddaughter, Nelly Custis Lewis, for breakfast George Washington "ate three small mush cakes [Indian meal] swimming in butter and honey, and drank three cups of tea without cream." The eighteenth-century recipe, as recounted in a letter, read, "if you wish to make 2½ quarts of flour up-take at night one quart of flour, five table spoonfuls of yeast and as much lukewarm water as will make it the consistency of pancake batter, mix it in a large stone pot and set it near a warm hearth (or a moderate fire) make it at candlelight and let it remain until the next morning then add the remaining quart and a half by degrees with a spoon when well mixed let it stand 15 or 20 minutes and then bake it—of this dough in the morning, beat up a white and half of the yolk of an egg—add as much lukewarm water as will make it like pancake batter, drop a spoonful at a time on a hoe or griddle (as we say in the south). When done on one side turn the other—the griddle must be rubbed in the first instance with a piece of beef suet or the fat of cold corned beef" (www.mountvernon.org/learn/explore_mv/index.cfm/pid/289; accessed March 8, 2010). The following recipe is more convenient for modern cooks:

8¾ C white cornmeal	3–4 C warm water (115 degrees)
¼ t yeast	shortening
1 egg, beaten	honey and butter

Mix 4 C white cornmeal with yeast and enough warm water to achieve a batter with the consistency of pancake batter. Cover and set aside overnight. The next morning, mix in the rest of the cornmeal, egg, and enough water to thin the batter. Cover and allow batter to rest 15–20 minutes. Heat shortening in frying pan or griddle. Spoon batter onto griddle, stirring before each batch is added to the pan. When the hoecake is browned on the bottom, flip and brown the other side. Serve drizzled with honey and melted butter.

Monticello Muffins

Of all of the early presidents, Jefferson was most enthusiastic about bees. He kept bees on his property and wrote extensively about them in Notes on Virginia:

> The honey bee is not a native of our country. Marcgrave, indeed, mentions a species of honey bee in Brazil. But this has no sting, and is therefore different from the one we have, which resembles perfectly that of Europe. The Indians concur with us in the tradition that it was brought from Europe, but when and by whom we know not. The bees have generally extended themselves into the country a little in advance of the settlers. The Indians, therefore, called them the white man's fly, and consider their approach as indicating the approach of the settlement of the whites. A question here occurs, How far northwardly have these insects been found? That they are unknown in Lapland, I infer from Scheffer's information, that the Laplanders eat the pine bark, prepared in a certain way, instead of those things sweetened with sugar. They eat this in place of things made with sugar. Certainly, if they had honey, it would be a better substitute for sugar than any preparation of the pine bark. Kalm tells us the honey bee cannot live through the winter in Canada. (www.monticello.org/jefferson/dayinlife/breakfst/fun.html; accessed March 8, 2010)

Among the "receipts" known to be used at Monticello, Jefferson's home, was one used by head cook Peter Hemings for "Monticello Muffins." No one could make them quite as he did, and, accordingly, the muffins were "a great luxury" for Jefferson. It is uncertain that he ate them with honey, but given his fondness for honey, it is likely that he did so. As Jefferson's granddaughter, Septimia Randolph Meikleham, recorded the recipe, "To a quart of flour put two table spoonsfull of yeast. Mix . . . the flour up with water so thin that the dough will stick to the table. Our cook takes it up and throws it down until it will no longer stick [to the table?] she puts it to rise until morning. In the morning she works the dough over . . . the first thing and makes it into little cakes like biscuit and sets them aside until it is time to back them. You know muffins are baked in a griddle in the hearth of the stove not inside. They bake very quickly. The second plate full is put on the fire when breakfast is sent in and they are ready by the time the first are eaten" (http://www.monticello .org/jefferson/dayinlife/breakfast/fun.html; accessed March 8, 2010).

A modern version is easier to prepare:

4 C flour	1½ packets of yeast
1½ C warm water	

Mix together flour, water, and yeast. Because the dough will be sticky, knead it after dusting your hands with flour—continue to add flour to dough until it is solid and no longer sticky. Cover dough with damp towel and leave overnight in a warm place, until it at least doubles in size. Form dough into balls approximately 1½ inches in diameter. Cover muffins with a damp towel and allow to rise for an hour.

Preheat ungreased cast-iron griddle over medium heat. Add shaped muffins to griddle and cook for about 5 minutes on each side. Serve immediately with melted butter and honey.

YIELDS ABOUT 2 DOZEN MUFFINS.

Mofo Tantely (Malagasy Honey Doughnut)

8 C all-purpose flour	1¼ C honey
2 t baker's yeast or baking soda	vegetable oil for frying
1 C water1 t salt	

Place the flour in a bowl and make a well in the middle. Add baker's yeast to 1 C lukewarm water, then pour into the well. Add salt, then knead by hand until the dough becomes soft. Wrap dough in a cloth for 3 hours. Make rings of dough. Heat oil, drop rings of dough into hot oil, a few at a time, and fry until brown. Meanwhile, warm the honey in a saucepan. Drop the browned doughnuts into the honey, remove and set aside on a plate, while frying the remaining dough. Serve doughnuts when cold.

Source: Maminarina Randrianadrasana, a University of Illinois at Urbana-Champaign graduate student in entomology from Antananarivo, Madagascar.

Sopaipilla (Fried Puff-Bread)

1¾ C flour	⅔ C milk
2 t baking powder	2 C vegetable oil
1 T sugar	honey
1 t salt	cinnamon-sugar mixture
2 T shortening	(1 t cinnamon per 1 T sugar)

Combine dry ingredients in a large mixing bowl. Cut in shortening with pastry blender or fork until mixture resembles cornmeal. Add milk, mixing just until dough holds together in a ball. Turn out onto a lightly floured surface; knead gently about 1 minute, until smooth. Cover dough and let rest for 1 hour.

Roll dough into a rectangle with floured rolling pin until 1/16 to ⅛ inch thick. Cut into 3-inch squares.

Heat oil in a saucepan to 370–380 degrees. Drop a few pieces of dough at a time into the oil, turning at once so they will puff evenly. Turn back over and brown both sides. Drain on absorbent paper towels. Serve hot, drizzled with honey and sprinkled with cinnamon-sugar mixture.

YIELDS ABOUT 20 SERVINGS.

Loukoumades (Greek Doughnuts)

Thyme honey would be regionally appropriate; it comes from hives in northern Greece and the Aegean Islands and is harvested in the summer months. The Sephardic Jewish version, bimuelos, are popular at Hanukkah, when tradition dictates eating food cooked with oil.

1 T yeast

1 C lukewarm milk

5½ C flour

1 t salt

1 egg, room temperature

1 C warm water

oil for frying

cinnamon

powdered sugar (optional)

Syrup
1 C honey

1 C sugar

½ C water

1 T lemon juice

Place yeast in warm milk and allow it to dissolve; let sit for 10–15 minutes. Sift together flour and salt. Make a well in the salt-flour mixture and add yeast solution and egg. Stir continuously while adding enough warm water to make a soft dough the consistency of pancake batter. Cover dough with a clean, damp cloth and allow to double in size.

While dough is rising, make syrup. Mix honey, sugar, and water in a saucepan; bring to boil and keep boiling for 6 minutes. Stir in lemon juice. Remove from heat but keep warm.

Heat oil in frying pan. Drop batter by the tablespoonful into hot oil; when the dough balls float and turn golden brown and puffy, remove them from the oil and allow to drain.

Pour syrup over doughnuts; sprinkle with cinnamon and powdered sugar if desired.

Pepero (Korean Fried Honey Sticks)

November 11 is celebrated in South Korea as Pepero Day because "11/11" is said to look like pepero sticks.

1 C flour, sifted

3 T sesame seed oil

3 T rice wine

2 T ginger juice

2 T honey

Syrup

1 C sugar

1 C water

2 T honey

½ t cinnamon

1½ t ground ginger

2 T pine nuts, finely minced

4 C vegetable oil for frying

Mix flour and sesame seed oil together thoroughly. In a separate bowl, combine liquids and add to the flour. Knead to dough-like consistency. Flatten dough into a square ½ inch thick and cut into long thin strips, then cut each strip into three even portions. Use a fork to poke holes into the sticks.

In a separate pan, make syrup by mixing sugar and water and boiling to reduce volume to 1 C. Cool slightly and add honey, cinnamon, and ground ginger.

Heat oil to 350–375 degrees. Deep fry dough until golden brown. Dip the cookies into the honey syrup, allowing it to soak through. Sprinkle with chopped pine nuts before serving.

Note: If you don't have ginger juice on hand, peel and grate fresh or frozen ginger root, and squeeze grated ginger through cheesecloth or a garlic press to extract the juice.

Yo-Yo (Tunisian Doughnuts)

4 eggs   zest of 1 orange
⅓ C sugar   3 C flour
¼ C vegetable oil   2 t baking powder
¼ C orange juice

Syrup
1 C sugar   ½ C honey
1 C water   2 C oil for frying
juice of ½ lemon

Mix eggs, sugar, oil, orange juice, and zest; beat for about 3 minutes. Add flour and baking powder gradually to form a soft, sticky dough. Allow to rest for 10 minutes. Create ropes approximately 1 inch thick and about 5 inches long. Pinch together the 2 ends to form a circle.

To make syrup, place sugar, water, and lemon juice in a saucepan and cook until liquid boils; continue to boil until syrup becomes sticky (about 5 minutes). Add honey and boil for another 5 minutes. Keep on low heat until doughnuts are ready to dip.

Heat oil to 350–375 degrees. Deep fry doughnuts until golden. Remove with tongs and dip in syrup. Serve immediately.

Chapter 8

Pies and Puddings

Curach

Bridget O'Neill sent this recipe from Ireland, where she works as a postdoctoral student. "Here's an Irish dessert recipe that I've seen a few different ways," she explains, "some without the rhubarb, some with strawberries instead of raspberries, but this version is the most common."

1½ C oatmeal
1 C rhubarb, chopped
2 C raspberries

3 T honey, divided
2 C heavy whipping cream
4 T whiskey

Preheat the oven to 400 degrees. Spread the oatmeal on a cookie sheet and bake until golden brown, stirring frequently. In a medium saucepan, add the rhubarb and half the raspberries with 2 T honey. Cook over medium heat until the rhubarb is tender. Let cool. In a large bowl, whip the cream until stiff. Fold in the remaining honey and whiskey. In a serving bowl, layer some of the whipped cream, some toasted oatmeal, the rhubarb mixture, and some fresh raspberries. Repeat. Garnish with fresh raspberries and serve at room temperature or chilled.

YIELDS 6 SERVINGS.

Washday Pudding

Washday pudding owes its name to its simplicity—it can be made even while at-tending to household chores.

Sauce

1 C brown sugar

2 C boiling water

2 T honey

2 T butter, melted

½ C sugar

Topping

½ C milk

1 T butter, melted

1 C flour

½ C sugar

1 t baking powder

½ t cinnamon

pinch of salt

1 C raisins

Mix together sauce ingredients and pour into a deep baking dish. Combine wet then dry topping ingredients and drop by large spoonful on top of sauce, like a cobbler. Bake at 350 degrees for 1 hour.

Quick Pumpkin Pudding

3 eggs

¾ C honey

½ t cinnamon

½ t ginger

½ t nutmeg

½ t salt

1¾ C pumpkin puree

1 C undiluted evaporated milk

Beat eggs lightly. Add honey, spices salt, and pumpkin. Mix well. Add undiluted evaporated milk. Butter or oil a deep 9-inch pie pan. Pour pumpkin mixture into pan. Bake at 325 degrees for 1 hour, or until knife blade comes out clean. Cool thoroughly before serving. Serve with honey-sweetened whipped cream if desired.

Source: Charlie Ott, of Ott's Honey, contributed this recipe to *A Book of Favorite Recipes,* compiled by the Central Illinois Tourism Council in 1988.

Prune Honey Pudding

1½ C prunes, pitted
1 C milk
1 C breadcrumbs
grated zest of ½ lemon
3 T honey

3 T butter or shortening, melted
1 C flour
2 t baking powder
1 t salt

Sauce

1 egg, beaten
1 C honey

2 t lemon juice

Cover prunes with warm water and let stand for 20 minutes. Drain and chop the pulp. Combine prunes with milk, breadcrumbs, lemon zest, honey, and melted butter. Sift together flour, baking powder, and salt; add to prune mixture and combine well. Place the mixture in a greased, covered mold (a 1-lb coffee can is excellent) in a kettle of boiling water that comes ⅔ to its top (place a weight on top of the mold). Cook for 2½ hours. Serve pudding with a sauce made by mixing together egg, honey, and lemon juice; heat slowly just to a boil, stirring constantly. Add hot water if a thinner sauce is desired.

Source: Adapted from *The All-American Cook Book,* 1922, page 106, in the Community Cookbook Collection of Hermilda Listeman (University of Illinois Library).

Honey Mousse

Rich and delicious.

4 eggs
1 C honey

1 envelope unflavored gelatin
2 C cream, whipped

Beat eggs slowly and pour over the honey. Put in double-boiler and cook slowly, stirring often until mixture thickens. Soften gelatin in a bit of cold water, add to honey mixture and stir until dissolved. Let mixture cool to room temperature, then fold in whipped cream. Put mixture into a mold, chill, and serve cold.

Gatnabour (Armenian Rice Pudding)

1½ C water
1 C rice
4 C milk
½ C honey

¼ C sugar
1 t vanilla
½ t cinnamon

Boil water and add rice; return water to a simmer and cook for 10 minutes. Add milk and simmer for another 30–40 minutes, or until mixture thickens. Add honey and sugar and bring to boil; simmer for 5 minutes. Remove from heat and stir in vanilla. Pour into individual dishes, chill, and sprinkle with cinnamon.

Cranberry Pudding with Honey Sauce

It is possible this pudding or a similar one was served in George Washington's time.

Pudding
2 C large cranberries
1½ C flour
1 t baking soda
½ t baking powder

½ t salt
⅔ C honey
⅓ C hot water

Honey Sauce
½ C butter
⅔ C honey
2 T flour

2 eggs, beaten slightly
½ C lemon juice
8 oz heavy cream

Mix cranberries with dry ingredients. Mix together honey and water and stir into fruit mixture. Pour the mixture into a heatproof bowl and set the bowl on a rack in about 1 inch of water in a large pot or kettle. Heat the water to a simmer, cover the pot, and steam the pudding for about 1 hour.

While the pudding is simmering, prepare sauce. In a double-boiler over simmering water, combine the butter, honey, flour, and eggs. Heat, stirring constantly until mixture thickens; do not boil. Remove from heat and stir in lemon juice and cream.

Source: Adapted from www.petri.house.gov/gw003.htm; accessed March 8, 2010.

Flan de miel (Honey Flan)

Flan is a popular dessert throughout Central and South America. This version from Mexico incorporates honey not only into the custard but also in the glaze, replacing the caramelized sugar.

3 eggs

1 C milk

½ C evaporated milk

½ C honey

1 t vanilla

¼ t cinnamon

Mix together eggs, milks, ¼ C honey, and vanilla. Divide the remaining honey into 6-oz ramekins, 1 T each. Pour the egg mixture into the ramekins, dividing equally among them. Position the ramekins in a baking pan and carefully add boiling water to the pan to a depth approximately ½ the height of the ramekins. Bake at 325 degrees for 35–45 minutes, or until custards are set. Allow to cool for 10–15 minutes, and then run a knife around the edge of the custards and invert onto plates. Sprinkle with cinnamon.

YIELDS 4 SERVINGS.

Nougatine glacée au miel de Provence

Nougatine is a hard candy, like brickle. Here it is combined with orange peel in a sweet confection from the south of France.

⅔ C sugar
¼ C slivered almonds
1 T oil
1⅔ C whipping cream

2 egg whites
5 T honey
½ C preserved orange peels, chopped

Combine sugar and almonds in saucepan, and sprinkle with a little water. Heat gently; when the sugar caramelizes, pour into a thin layer on an oiled plate. Allow to cool and harden (approximately 20 minutes). Once it has hardened, break the nougat into small pieces and reserve. Whip the cream until stiff peaks form. Whip the egg whites until stiff peaks form, then drizzle in the honey. Combine whipped cream and egg whites, and stir in nougat and orange peels. Pour mixture into 6 ramekins and chill for 2 hours or more.

YIELDS 6 SERVINGS.

Hangop with Blackberries, Honey, and Mint

"The Netherlands," says Marianne Alleyne, who is Dutch, "is not known for its cuisine (my husband claims that we had to colonize far away places to get decent food). This is an example of an old-fashioned recipe. Hangop (curd) is made with dairy, usually yogurt but also buttermilk and biest (the first milk from the cow after the birth of the calf). The dairy product is hung inside a dishcloth. Traditionally, hangop is eaten with cripcakes (biscuits), sugar and cinnamon, or berry juice. Here the hangop is sweetened with blackberries and honey and a little mint is added."

2 pt whole yogurt
3⅓ C blackberries
3 T vodka (optional)

honey to taste
a few sprigs of mint

Place a clean, rinsed dishtowel in a colander. Suspend the colander over a pot and pour the yogurt into the dishcloth. Leave the yogurt "hanging" for at least 3 hours but preferably overnight. One hour prior to serving, clean the blackberries and soak them in the vodka (drain before serving). Spoon the hangop (drained yogurt in the dishtowel) into a serving bowl, and mix with honey (the amount depends on your sweet tooth and the sourness of the berries). Sprinkle the mint over the blackberries. Serve the hangop with the blackberries alongside or combine hangop and blackberries together.

Source: Marianne Alleyne is a research assistant professor in the
Department of Entomology at the University of Illinois at Urbana-Champaign.

Risengrynsgrøt (Norwegian Rice Custard)

Puddings are very common in Norwegian cuisine; my cousin Jonathan Strauch, an ophthalmologist in Norway, introduced me to rømmegrøt, a lovely sour cream pudding served warm. Risengrynsgrøt, a little lighter, is a popular winter dish. Although Norway imports much of its honey, honey bees have been there since the thirteenth century. A. C. Hanson published his Veiledning I ensiktsmessig biavl, *a Norwegian beekeeping guide, in 1844. Such wildflowers as the tormentil (*Potentilla tormentilla*) and wood avens (*Geum urbanum*) are important nectar sources for home-grown honey.*

4 eggs, slightly beaten	¾ C cooked rice (cooked without salt)
4 C whole milk, scalded	¼ C raisins (optional)
¼ C sugar	1 T butter
¼ C honey	ground cardamom
1 t vanilla	cinnamon

In a large bowl, combine eggs, milk, sugar, honey, and vanilla. Stir in cooked rice and raisins (optional); mix well. Pour into a 1-inch-deep baking dish and dot top with butter; sprinkle with ground cardamom. Set baking dish in pan of water and put both into the oven. Bake at 350 degrees for 25 minutes; sprinkle cinnamon on top and continue baking for another 20 minutes. Pudding is done if top jiggles when shaken.

Honey and Curd (Mel i mató)

Mel i mató is one of the emblematic desserts in Catalonia in northeastern Spain. Mató, a fresh cheese made from cow's or goat's milk with no salt added, is similar to ricotta or curd cheese. It is usually served with honey. The recipe for mató appears in medieval cookbooks, and it is still traditional to obtain it from monasteries in Catalonia such as Monestir de Montserrat.

4 C goat's milk or cow's milk	water
1 package rennet powder (see Note)	honey

Place the milk in a pot and heat to boil. Meanwhile, mix the rennet powder with water. After milk boils, remove the pot from the heat and cool to 160 degrees. Add 4 T of the rennet mixture and let sit until it cools completely. Strain the milk into a bowl carefully with a very fine sieve or a cloth napkin, making sure all the whey is drained from the milk container. Curd can be kept in the refrigerator for approximately 8 days. Serve a portion of curd covered with honey.

Note: The milk can also be curdled with vinegar or vegetable rennet such as cardoon (*Cynara cardunculus*) instead of rennet powder.

Source: Eva Castells, from Barcelona, is a former postdoctoral associate in the Department of Entomology at the University of Illinois at Urbana-Champaign.

Gram Bea's Saskatoon Pie

"This is from my grandmother who pioneered on the prairies of Alberta," says Janet Sperling. "Honey was used for special occasions while white sugar was more commonly used since it was cheaper." Any good pastry recipe will work, but I like the following.

Never-Fail Pastry

5 C flour	1 egg
2 C shortening	water
1 T brown sugar	white vinegar
1 t baking soda	

Saskatoon Filling

freshly picked or frozen Saskatoon berries [service berries] to fill the pie shell

generous amount of honey

To make pie crust, cut shortening into flour mixed with brown sugar and baking soda. In a cup, place 1 egg and beat, then fill the cup to ⅔ with water and then ¾ with vinegar. Make a well in the center of the flour, add liquid, and mix carefully. This makes several pies, and the remaining dough can be frozen in pie plates.

To make filling, mix berries and honey. Pour into lined pie shell. Cover with pastry top, and crimp edges. The pie should be baked until crispy and lightly browned, about 50 minutes.

Source: Janet Sperling is married to Felix Sperling, an entomologist at the University of Alberta, Edmonton.

Cinnamon and Honey Pastry Wedges

pastry for double-
  crust pie (9 inch)
1 T butter, melted
2 T honey

1 T sugar
1 t cinnamon
¼ C pecans or walnuts,
  finely chopped

Divide pastry in half and roll each half into a 10-inch circle. Transfer to 2 ungreased 12-inch pizza pans. Score pastry into wedges (do not cut through). Mix melted butter and honey; brush onto rounds. Sprinkle with sugar, cinnamon, and pecans. Bake at 350 degrees for 15–18 minutes, or until edges are golden brown. Cut pastry along scored lines; immediately remove from pan. Serve warm.

YIELDS 2 DOZEN WEDGES.

Super-Duper Cheesecake

This was my mother's favorite cheesecake recipe; not the typical New York–style cheesecake, it's based on cottage cheese rather than cream cheese.

Crust

1 C zwieback toast crumbs   ¼ C melted butter
2 T sugar

Filling

3 eggs, separated   ½ t salt
2 C reduced-fat sour cream   ¼ C sifted flour
1 t vanilla   2¼ C creamed cottage cheese
1 T lemon juice   ¼ C sugar
½ C honey

Mix zwieback crumbs and sugar. Add melted butter and blend completely. Press mixture firmly along sides and bottom of a 9-inch spring-form pan or round cake pan at least 3 inches deep.

Separate eggs; set the egg whites aside in a deep bowl for beating. In a blender container, add all ingredients except the sugar and reserved egg whites. Cover and blend for about 1 minute, scrape down sides of blender with a rubber spatula, and blend another minute until mixture is smooth.

Beat egg whites until foamy, then add sugar, 1 T at a time, and beat in quickly. Egg whites should form soft peaks; do not over-beat. Using a spatula, gently fold the blended cottage cheese mixture into the beaten whites. Pour into the crumb-lined pan. Bake in a slow (325 degrees) oven about 1¼ hours until cake is set in center. Let cake get completely cold before cutting or removing from pan. It will sink slightly.

Melopita (Greek Ricotta and Honey Pie)

This traditional Easter dessert in Greece is thought to have originated on the Island of Siphnos. This version was suggested by Katherine DeLucia. This pie can be made with or without the pastry crust.

Sesame Seed Pastry

1 C flour
⅓ C butter, room temperature
1 T sugar

1 T sesame seeds, toasted
¼ t salt

Filling

15 oz whole milk ricotta cheese
2 eggs
½ C sugar
½ C honey

½ C heavy cream
1 t grated lemon zest
¼ t nutmeg
¼ t cinnamon

To make pastry crust, blend together all ingredients; press into an 8-inch pie pan. Prick dough all over, and bake at 475 degrees for 5 minutes.

To make filling: combine all filling ingredients and beat until light. Pour into baked pie crust (optional). Bake at 350 degrees for 40–50 minutes until firm. Store in refrigerator until serving. Yields 10–12 servings.

Pumpkin Honey Pie

1½ C pumpkin puree
½ C honey
½ C brown sugar
½ t cinnamon
½ t salt

¼ t nutmeg
¼ t ginger
¼ t allspice
2 eggs, beaten
1 C evaporated milk

Combine all ingredients and beat until thoroughly blended. Pour into a 9-inch pie shell. Bake at 400 degrees for 10 minutes, then turn temperature down to 325 degrees and continue to bake for about 40–50 minutes, until filling is set.

Source: Adapted from *Honey: It's Nutritious and Delicious,* a brochure published by the Illinois State Beekeepers Association.

Banbury Tarts

1 C raisins, chopped	2 T lemon juice
½ C sugar	2 t grated lemon zest
¼ C honey	¼ C finely chopped walnuts
¼ C graham cracker crumbs	pastry for a double-crust, 9-inch pie
1 egg	

Combine all filling ingredients. Roll pie pastry thin and cut into 3-inch squares. Place 1 t filling mix in the center of each square; fold into a triangle and press edges together with a fork to seal. Prick with a fork to allow steam to escape (or, alternatively, cut slit in the top of each tart). Place triangles on a greased baking sheet. Bake at 400 degrees for 13–15 minutes until lightly browned. Remove from oven and cool on wire racks.

Source: Adapted from *Old Favorite Honey Recipes,* a booklet published by the American Honey Institute, Madison, Wisconsin, in 1941.

Coventry Tartlets

1¾ C cottage cheese or cream cheese	½ t salt
½ C honey	¼ t nutmeg
¼ C butter	1 T orange juice
2 egg yolks	pastry for a double-crust, 9-inch pie

Combine all filling ingredients, beating to a smooth, creamy consistency. Line 12 individual tart molds with pastry. Prick pastry, and fill with cheese filling. Bake at 450 degrees for 10 minutes; reduce heat to 325 degrees and bake until golden brown and firm. Remove from oven and cool. Garnish with "red or green honey jelly."

Source: Adapted from *Old Favorite Honey Recipes,* a booklet published by the American Honey Institute, Madison, Wisconsin, in 1941.

Honey Pies

Here is a recipe for a honey pie crust, and seven different filling options. Bake the following pies at 425 degrees for 12 minutes, then reduce temperature to 350 degrees and bake approximately 15–20 minutes.

Double-Crust Pie Dough

5–6 T milk

1½ T honey

1 t salt

1 C shortening

2¾ C flour

Mix milk and honey; dissolve salt in liquid. Cut shortening into flour and blend until pea-sized clumps are obtained. Pour in the liquid and mix until dough is uniform. Divide dough in half, roll out, and cut to fit pan. If baked before filling, prick bottom with fork and bake at 450 degrees for 8–10 minutes.

Option 1: Honey Pecan Pie (Single Crust)

2 C pecans, chopped

3 eggs, beaten but not foamy

2 C light honey

1 t vanilla

4 T butter, melted

½ t salt

Option 2: Honey Pumpkin Pie (Single Crust)

1½ C pumpkin puree

¾ C honey

1 t cinnamon

½ t ginger

½ t salt

3 eggs, beaten

½ C milk

½ C cream or evaporated milk

Option 3: Honey Cherry Pie (Double Crust)

1 can (21 oz) pie cherries

¼ t salt

3 T cornstarch

¾ C honey

1 T butter

¼ t almond extract

Option 4: Crunchy-Top Apricot Prune Pie (Single Crust)

2¾ C mixed pitted prunes
    and apricots, cut into
    small pieces
1 egg, beaten
¼ C honey

dash of salt
juice of 1 lemon
1 t lemon zest
½ C orange juice
dash of nutmeg

Topping
¼ C butter, melted
3 T honey
⅓ C flour

¼ C raw rolled oats
¼ t cinnamon
dash of salt

Option 5: Honey Raisin Pie (Double Crust)

1 C orange juice
1 T grated orange peel
4 T lemon juice
¾ C honey
½ t salt

1½ C raisins
4 T cornstarch
¾ C cold water
2 T butter

Boil together orange juice, peel, lemon juice, honey, salt, and ½ C water. Dissolve cornstarch in remaining water, add to hot mixture, and stir until thickened. Add raisins. Pour into pie shell, dot with butter, top with crust, and crimp edges to seal.

Option 6: Honey Apple Pie (Double Crust)

5 C sliced apples
¾ C honey
1 T cinnamon

1 t vanilla
2 T butter to dot on top of apples

Option 7: Peaches and Honey Cream Pie (Single Crust)

1 large can peaches, drained
1 C sour cream
2 eggs, beaten lightly

pinch of salt
¼ C mild honey
1 t vanilla

Place peach slices in pie shell. Combine remaining ingredients and pour over peaches.

Honey-Lemon Pie

Pie Dough

1 C flour	½ t salt
⅛ t grated lemon zest	¼ C butter
¼ t sugar	2–3 T cold water

Filling

¾ C flour	½ C butter, melted
¼ t salt	⅓ C milk
1 t baking soda	¼ C lemon juice
1 C sugar	1 t grated lemon zest
3 eggs	1 C honey

To make pastry shell, mix together flour, lemon zest, sugar, and salt. With a pastry blender or fork, cut in butter until pieces are rice-sized. Add a few drops of water and mix with fork until water is distributed evenly. Roll on floured surface into a 10-inch circle. Place in a 9-inch pie pan and flute edges. Refrigerate while filling is prepared.

To make filling, combine flour, salt, sugar, and baking soda. In separate bowl, beat eggs until thick; blend in butter, milk, lemon juice, lemon zest, and honey. Stir in dry ingredients, mix well, and pour into unbaked refrigerated pastry shell. Bake at 325 degrees for 55–60 minutes; remove from oven and cool. Refrigerate for at least 1 hour before serving.

Strawberry Rhubarb Crisp

Fruit

4 C rhubarb cut into
   ½-inch pieces
2 C strawberries, sliced

½ C honey
1 T cornstarch

Topping

1 C flour
½ C old-fashioned oats
   (not quick or instant oats)
½ C brown sugar

½ t cinnamon
¼ C slivered almonds
⅓ C butter, melted

Place sliced rhubarb into a greased 9-inch-square pan. Layer strawberries on top. In a small bowl, mix together honey and cornstarch. Drizzle over fruit. In a medium bowl stir together flour, oats, brown sugar, cinnamon, and almonds. Stir in melted butter. Mix until combined and crumbly. Sprinkle evenly over fruit. Bake at 350 degrees for 50 minutes until fruit is bubbly and top is golden brown. Serve warm or at room temperature.

SERVES 6.

Peach Honey Cobbler

8 C peaches
¼ C honey
3 T lemon juice
¼ C flour

½ t nutmeg
⅛ t cinnamon
¼ t salt
2 T butter

Biscuit

1 C flour
1½ t baking powder
1 T honey

½ t salt
3 T butter
½ C milk

Stir together peaches, honey, lemon juice, flour, cinnamon, nutmeg, and salt. Let stand 15 minutes and then place in a 9 by 13-inch pan. Dot with butter. Make biscuits by mixing flour, baking powder, honey, and salt. Using a pastry blender, blend in butter; stir in milk. Mix until dough comes together to make a ball. Drop by spoonful onto the fruit mixture. Bake at 400 degrees for 25–30 minutes, or until brown and puffy.

Apple Honey Crisp

A recipe adapted from the National Honey Board's brochure Recipes with Honey: Nature's Sweetener. *The board is located in Firestone, Colorado, where a multitude of wildflowers provide nectar for honey bees.*

5 C apples, quartered and sliced	½ t nutmeg
¾ C honey (divided)	1 C flour
1 t cinnamon	¼ C butter, softened

Nutmeg Cream

½ C whipping cream	2 T butter
2 T honey	¼ t nutmeg

Toss apple slices with ½ C honey, cinnamon, and nutmeg. Pour apple mixture into 2-quart baking dish. In separate bowl, mix flour with butter and ¼ C honey until crumbs form; scatter flour mixture over apples. Bake at 350 degrees for 40–45 minutes, or until topping is golden brown. Remove from oven and cool slightly.

To make cream topping, combine all ingredients in a saucepan and bring to boil; lower heat and simmer until mixture thickens (about 5 minutes). Spoon warm cream over crisp.

Chapter 9

Cakes

Lekach (Rosh Hashanah Honey Cake)

Although Israel is described as the "land of milk and honey" in the Book of Exodus, rabbinical scholars, including Norman Klein of Sinai Temple, in Champaign, Illinois, have long maintained that the "honey" was not bee-derived but rather syrup from date palms. An archaeological discovery at Tel Rehov in Israel restores bee-derived honey to its rightful place. An excavation unearthed evidence of more than a hundred cylindrical clay beehives from the First Temple period, stacked just as depicted in Egyptian tomb hieroglyphics. This particular honey cake is traditionally made with buckwheat honey, which is very strong and dark. The taste of buckwheat honey, for me, says L'shanah Tovah! (Happy New Year).

4 eggs	2 t baking powder
¾ C sugar	1 t baking soda
½ C vegetable oil	½ t each cinnamon and allspice
1 C honey	1 T instant coffee powder
1 t vanilla	dissolved in 1 C hot water
3 C sifted flour	(or 1 C strong black coffee)
½ t salt	slivered or sliced almonds for topping

Beat eggs until frothy and add sugar, oil, honey, and vanilla. In separate bowl, combine flour with salt, baking powder, baking soda, and spices. Add dry ingredients to egg mixture alternately with coffee, mixing only until blended (do not over-mix). Pour batter into a greased and floured 12-C Bundt pan, or two 9-inch loaf pans, or one 9 by 13-inch pan. Bake at 325 degrees for 50 minutes, or until cake tests done. Cool 10–15 minutes, remove from pan, and place on wire rack to continue cooling. Top with almonds.

Source: Berenbaum family recipe.

Sally's Honey Cake

3 eggs	2 t vanilla
1 C buckwheat honey	2¾ C flour
¾ C sugar	½ t allspice
1 C warm coffee	¾ t cinnamon
2 t baking soda	1 t ginger
½ C vegetable oil	1 t ground cloves
2 t baking powder	2 t whiskey

Beat eggs and honey together. Add sugar and mix again. Mix baking soda into coffee, then add with oil to egg mixture. Add remaining ingredients and beat together well. Pour batter into greased tube pan. Bake at 325 degrees for 55 minutes.

Source: Sally Heckelman is the sister of Gene Robinson, an internationally renowned expert on honey bee biology at the University of Illinois at Urbana-Champaign.

Scripture Cake (Old Testament Version)

Scripture cakes were very popular in the early twentieth century; all ingredients were identified by biblical references. Honey appears frequently in scripture cake recipes, not surprisingly given how frequently honey is mentioned in the Bible. The description of Israel as a "land flowing with milk and honey" appears 21 times in the Old Testament (Exod. 3:8, 3:17, 13:5, 33:3; Lev. 30:35; Num. 13:28, 14:8, 16:14; Deut. 6:3, II:9, 26:15, 27:3, 31:20; Jos. 5:6; Tob. 30:17; Jer. II:5, 32:2; Ezek. 20:6, 30:15; Sirach 46:10; and Baruch I:20).

1 C Judges 5:25 (1 C butter)	1 C Genesis 24:17 (1 C water)
2 C Jeremiah 6:20 (2 C sugar)	2 C 1 Samuel 30:12 (2 C raisins)
1 large T Exodus 16:31	2 C 1 Samuel 30:12
(1 T honey)	(2 C dried figs, chopped)
6 Isaiah 10:14 (6 eggs)	1 C Genesis 43:11)
3½ C 1 Kings 4:22 (3½ C flour)	(1 C almonds, sliced
sweet 1 Kings 10:2 to taste	pinch Leviticus 2:13 (pinch salt)
(spices to taste)	

Follow Solomon's advice for making good boys (Proverbs 3:14), and you will have a good cake (thou shalt beat him with the rod, and shalt deliver his soul from hell).

Cream butter, sugar, add honey, and then beat in eggs 1 at a time. Sift together flour and spices; add to egg mixture, alternating with water. Fold in raisins, figs, and almonds and stir until well blended. Place batter in 2 greased 9 by 5 by 3-inch loaf pans. Bake at 325 degrees for 55–60 minutes, or until test toothpick comes out clean. Cool thoroughly in pans before inverting onto racks to complete cooling.

Source: Adapted from a recipe contributed by Mrs. Milton L. Ducker to the *Peoria Women's Cookbook,* 1915, prepared by the Peoria, Illinois, First Methodist Episcopal Church's Young Women's League, in the Community Cookbook Collection of Hermilda Listeman (University of Illinois Library).

Scripture Cake (Old and New Testaments)

Although this recipe pulls honey from the Old Testament, references to honey do appear in the New Testament. Jesus received broiled fish and honeycomb the day of his resurrection (Luke 24:42), and John the Baptist subsisted on "locusts and honey" during his sojourn in the wilderness (Mark 1:6, Matt. 3:4). The ingredients for this scripture cake are the same as for the previous recipe except that leavening is used in this one.

1 C Judges 5:25 (1 C butter)	pinch Leviticus 2:13 (pinch salt)
2 C Jeremiah 6:20 (2 C sugar)	1 Kings 10:10 to taste (spices to taste)
6 Isaiah 10:14 (6 eggs)	1 C Genesis 24:17 (1 C water)
3½ C 1 Kings 4:22 (3½ C flour)	1 T Exodus 16:21 (1 T honey)
½ T Matthew 13:33	2 C 1 Samuel 30:12 (2 C raisins)
(½ T baking soda)	2 C 2 Samuel 30:12 (2 C figs)
1 t Matthew 13:33	1 C Genesis 43:11 (1 C almonds)
(1 t cream of tartar)	

Follow Proverbs 23:13, Father Solomon's advice for making good boys (Thou shalt beat him with the rod, and shalt deliver his soul from hell).

Cream together butter and sugar, beat in eggs 1 at a time, beating well after each one. Sift together flour, baking soda, cream of tartar, salt, and spices. Add dry ingredients alternately with water to creamed mixture. Stir in honey, fold in raisins, figs, and almonds. Mix well. Turn into two well-greased 9 by 5 by 3-inch loaf pans. Bake at 325 degrees for about 60 minutes, making sure not to over-bake, until loaves test done by the toothpick test. Let cool for 30 minutes in pans before turning out onto rack.

Source: Adapted from Mrs. T. W. Meserve, *A Book of Dorcas Dishes: Family Recipes,* 1911, contributed by the Dorcas Society of Hollis and Buxton, Maine, in the Community Cookbook Collection of Hermilda Listeman (University of Illinois Library).

Honey Devil's Food Cake

"Sweepstakes over all cakes" at the Illinois State Fair 1934 ("this is an institute recipe"):

½ C butter	2½ C cake flour
¾ C honey	½ t salt
½ C sugar	½ t baking soda
1 egg, separated	2 t baking powder
2 squares bitter chocolate, melted	¾ C milk

Cream butter, honey, and sugar thoroughly; add egg yolk and melted chocolate. Add dry ingredients, alternating with milk. Beat egg whites until stiff; fold into batter. Pour into greased cake pans. Bake at 350 degrees for 45–50 minutes.

Honey Fudge Cake

Custard Mixture
1 C grated bitter chocolate

1 egg yolk

½ C brown sugar

½ C mild honey (e.g., clover)

Cake Mixture
½ C mild honey

½ C brown sugar

⅓ C shortening, melted

2 egg yolks, beaten

½ C milk

2 C flour

1 t baking soda

3 egg whites

Honey Fudge Icing
2 C powdered sugar

5 T cocoa

1 t salt

1 T butter, melted

3 T mild honey

3 T whipping cream

6 T cream or milk

To make custard, in a saucepan, stir together all ingredients except honey. Heat slowly, stirring constantly. When thoroughly mixed, remove from heat and stir in honey. Set aside to cool.

To make cake, combine sugar and honey, then stir in melted shortening. Stir in egg yolks, add milk, then add flour. Stir in the cooled custard mixture. Dissolve baking soda in a little warm water, and add to mixture. Lastly, beat egg whites stiffly, and fold into mixture. Pour batter into well-greased round cake pans. Bake at 375 degrees for 15–20 minutes. Frost when cool.

To make frosting, sift dry ingredients together. Mix butter and honey together, and add to sugar mixture. Stir in whipped cream and then mix in the milk or cream. Stir vigorously until light and fluffy.

Source: Vern Milum for National Honey Week, archives of the
Department of Entomology, University of Illinois at Urbana-Champaign.

Yellow Honey Cake

Second prize in the 1934 Illinois State Fair Honey Culinary Competition.

½ C butter
1¼ C sugar
¾ C honey
1 C milk

3 eggs, well beaten
2 C flour
4 t baking powder

Cream butter, sugar, and honey. Add milk and eggs. Then sift in flour with baking powder and "beat, beat, beat." Pour into greased cake pans. Bake at 350 degrees until done.

Source: Adapted from the *Annual Report of the Illinois State Beekeepers Association*, 1934.

Wartime Honey Cake

The pamphlet in which this appeared, published in Great Britain in 1943, offered tips for cooking in times of emergency, including "how to save your dinner if air-raids come," stretching and shrinking family meals, saving scraps, and "making the most of tinned food." This honey cake recipe appeared in the chapter titled "Cakes with Less Fruit and Alternatives to Sugar," a commodity in short supply in wartime England.

2 C self-rising flour
pinch of salt
6 T margarine

¾ C candied peel
1 large egg, beaten in ¼ pint milk
3 T honey

Brush a cake pan with melted margarine and dust with flour. Sieve the flour and salt into a basin, rub in the margarine. Add the chopped peel, stir in the egg and milk, add the honey, and beat well. Put into the prepared tin and bake in a moderate oven [350 degrees] for 1 hour.

Source: Susan Croft, *The Stork Wartime Cookery Book* (London: Stork Magazine Co., Unilever House, 1943).

Meekook (Estonian Honey Cake)

I received a copy of the cookbook that is the source of this recipe from a high-school friend, Paul Luedig, who grew up to become a diplomat for the Mission of Estonia to the United Nations.

1 C honey	½ C cold espresso coffee
3 C flour	1 orange (juice and grated peel)
1 t baking soda	1 t vanilla 2 T butter
1 t baking powder	1 C sugar
1 t cinnamon	4 eggs, separated
½ t cardamom	1 C chopped walnuts
¼ t salt	

Bring the honey to a boil and then cool. Combine the flour with the dry ingredients. Mix espresso, orange juice and grated peel, and vanilla together. Cream the butter with the sugar. Add egg yolks, one by one, and then stir in the honey. Add dry ingredients to the honey mixture alternately with the espresso mixture. Beat egg whites until stiff, and fold into batter; gently stir in chopped walnuts. Pour the batter into a well-greased cake pan. Bake at 325 degrees for 50 minutes, or until done. Remove cake from pan and cool.

Adapted from Hilja Jukkum, Toronto, Canada, in Vilvi Plirisild, *The Estonian Cookbook: Traditional Estonian Recipes Donated by Estonian Women in the United States and Canada* (Los Angeles: Los Angelese Eesti Naisklubi, 1976).

French Honey Loaf

Auvergne was a historical province in south central France that today corresponds to the departements of Puy-de-Dome, Cantal, Haute-Loire, and Allier. Among the chief agricultural products are lentils, barley, and sunflowers. Sunflower honey would thus be a good choice for this honey-flavored loaf.

1¾ C flour
1 t baking soda
½ C sugar
½ C milk

4 T acacia or sunflower honey
6 T butter, melted
2–4 whole star anise pods

Mix together flour, baking soda, and sugar; make a depression in the center and pour in milk, honey, and butter. Stir until blended. Place the star anise pods in the bottom of a greased and floured loaf pan and gently pour in batter. Bake at 350 degrees for 40 minutes, or until knife inserted into cake comes away clean. Cool the cake in the pan and unmold when cool.

Tiessennau Mel (Welsh Honey Muffin Cakes)

½ C butter
½ C brown sugar
1 egg, separated
½ C honey
1 C flour

1 t cinnamon
½ t baking soda
¼ C milk
confectioner's sugar

Cream the butter and sugar until light. Beat in egg yolk and honey gradually. Combine flour with cinnamon and baking soda; add to butter mixture, alternating with milk. Beat egg white until stiff and fold into batter. Fill muffin tins halfway and sprinkle confectioner's sugar on top. Bake at 400 degrees for 20 minutes. Cool and top muffins with more confectioner's sugar if desired.

Jemný Perník (Czech Honey Cake)

To make the spice mix for this flavorful cake, combine 2 t cinnamon, 2 t cloves, 2 t allspice, 4 t anise, 4 t star anise, and 1 grated vanilla bean. If you don't want to grate a vanilla bean, use vanilla sugar or 1 t vanilla extract instead. Apple pie or gingerbread spice mix is also a good substitute.

2½ C flour
1 C sugar
½ t baking soda
8 T spice mix
⅔ C honey
¼ C milk
2 egg yolks, lightly beaten

1 T rum (optional)
1 t each grated lemon peel
    and orange peel
½ C raisins (or substitute
    golden raisins or currants)
½ C blanched almonds, chopped
½ C walnuts, chopped

Sift dry ingredients into a bowl. In a saucepan, heat honey to lukewarm and add milk, egg yolks, rum, and grated lemon and orange peel. Pour honey mixture into dry ingredients and beat to smooth soft dough. Mix in raisins, almonds, and walnuts. Let batter sit, covered, for 10–12 hours in a cool place. Grease a jellyroll pan, and spread dough evenly. Bake at 325 degrees for 30 minutes.

Rum Cake (Bizcocho de Ron)

¼ lb butter, softened
¼ C brown sugar
¼ C honey
2 eggs
¼ C water

½ C dark rum or spiced rum
2 C flour, sifted
2½ t baking powder
¼ t salt
confectioner's sugar for garnish

Cream butter and sugar in a large bowl. Add the honey, eggs, water, and rum; mix well. In another bowl, combine cake flour, baking powder, and salt. Pour dry ingredients over butter mixture and beat well to combine all ingredients. Pour the batter into a greased 8-inch round pan at 350 degrees for 30 minutes, or until tester comes out clean. Let cake cool in pan or on a cooling rack. To serve, invert cake on platter. Trim top if uneven. Sift confectioner's sugar over top.

SERVES 8.

Adrienne's Karidopeta (Greek Nut Cake)

This is a reconstruction of the Greek nut cake that my mother, Adrienne Berenbaum, used to bake on occasion. As I recall, the recipe came from the women's auxiliary of a Greek Orthodox church in Mercer County, N.J. The group would sell these and other pastries at the annual Mercer Hospital Horse Show.

Syrup

¾ C honey	1 lemon peel
¾ C water	

Cake

1 C butter	1 C farina (or Cream of Wheat)
1 C sugar	1 T baking powder
6 eggs	1 t cinnamon
1 C flour	1 C walnuts, chopped

Make syrup first by combining ingredients in a pot and bringing them to a boil. Boil 10 minutes, stirring occasionally. Allow to cool. To make cake, cream butter and sugar; add eggs 1 at a time, beating constantly. Add flour, farina, baking powder, and cinnamon and beat well. Mix in walnuts. Pour batter in a greased 9 by 13-inch pan. Bake at 350 degrees for 30 minutes. Pour cooled syrup over cake while cake is hot. Allow cake to cool, then cut into diamond shapes. Cake slices can be placed individually in cupcake liners and topped with a maraschino cherry.

Chocolate Honey Cake

Adapted by Kim Walden from The Enchanted Broccoli Forest by Mollie Katzen. Kim, a technician in the University of Illinois Department of Entomology, first made this cake for an Entomology Graduate Student Association fundraiser. The recipe works better, she says, if the honey is whipped separately with an electric mixer until it is opaque; whipping air into the honey helps lighten the cake.

½ C butter, softened

1 square unsweetened chocolate

¾ C light-colored honey

2 eggs

1 t vanilla

¼ C unsweetened cocoa

1 C unbleached all-purpose flour

½ t salt

1½ t baking powder

1 C chocolate chips

nonstick spray for the pan

Melt butter and chocolate together over low heat; remove from heat and cool. Beat honey in mixing bowl until opaque (approximately 2 minutes). Add eggs and beat well. Mix in vanilla. In a separate bowl, sift all dry ingredients. Pour the melted chocolate/butter mixture into the dry ingredients and stir to combine. Stir in chocolate chips, and mix thoroughly. Pour batter into a greased 9-inch loaf pan. Bake at 350 degrees for 25–30 minutes, or until a toothpick inserted into the center comes away clean.

SERVES 6 TO 8.

Medovnik (Russian Honey Cake)

Medovnik is a moist, delicate cake made with thin layers and custard. It apparently is quite popular in the Ukraine, Russia, and the Czech Republic.

1 C sugar
2 eggs, beaten
¼ C butter

2 T buckwheat honey
2 t baking powder
3 C all-purpose flour

Cream Filling

1 14-oz can sweetened
   condensed milk (or
   sour cream)

3 eggs, beaten
2 T honey
¼ C butter

Crumb Topping

½ C sugar
1 T honey

2½–3 C crushed cookie crumbs

Preheat oven to 375 degrees. Cut 5 rounds of parchment paper into 8-inch circles. In a small bowl, combine sugar and eggs; set aside. Melt the butter in a large saucepan over low heat. Add honey, egg-sugar mixture, and baking powder; stir constantly until well blended and foamy. Remove from heat. Add flour and stir until dough is not sticky (if sticky, add additional flour).

Separate dough into 5 equal pieces and place on the parchment paper circles; cover each with plastic wrap to keep pliable. Using a floured rolling pin, roll each portion into a circle ¼ inch thick (dimensions don't matter, but the thickness does). Place on floured cookie sheet and bake 3–5 minutes, or until just barely golden but not brown (watch it carefully). Remove from baking sheet and cool on a wire rack. Repeat with the remaining 4 sections of the dough, flouring cookie sheet as necessary.

To make the custard filling, in a large saucepan over medium heat, combine sweetened condensed milk, eggs, honey, and butter. Stirring constantly, bring to a boil; simmer until mixture thickens. Remove from heat and cool.

To assemble cake, alternate layers of cake with cream filling on a large serving dish, applying the filling liberally. Top the cake by crumbling the fifth layer of cake into small pieces and sprinkling them over the last layer of custard. Mix crumb topping ingredients and sprinkle over cake. Let the cake sit 6 to 8 hours before serving.

YIELDS 1 CAKE.

Spiced Honey Cake Cockaigne

This receipe is from Bettina Francis, a professor of entomology at the University of Illinois at Urbana-Champaign, who says she hasn't made it in over 25 years, "but it was good when I did. However, it is hard to mix—the dough is very heavy and sticky. It's a spice cake; very dense and tastes somewhat like Lebkuchen, although the texture is different. It keeps for weeks and should be aged at least 3 days before eating (but as far as I remember, it is also good right away)."

¼ C honey	½ t cloves
¾ C water	⅛ t cardamom
½ C sugar	¼ C pecans or blanched
2 C rye flour	slivered almonds
½ t baking soda	1 T grated orange zest
2 t baking powder	¼–½ C finely chopped
1 T cinnamon	citron, or candied ginger
½ t allspice	

Heat honey, water, and sugar in a double-boiler until small bubbles appear. Remove from the heat. In a separate bowl, combine flour, baking soda, baking powder, cinnamon, allspice, cloves, and cardamom. Add honey mixture to dry ingredients and beat with electric mixer for 10 minutes. Stir in nuts, orange zest, and citron. Pour batter into a greased 9-inch loaf pan. Place pan in oven and add a pan of water on bottom rack of the oven. Bake at 350 degrees for 1 hour.

YIELDS 1 LOAF.

Quick Coffee Cake

1½ C sifted flour
2 t baking powder
½ t salt
1 egg

⅔ C milk
⅓ C honey
3 t melted butter

Honey Topping
¼ t butter
¼ C sugar
¼ C sifted flour

¼ C honey
¼ C chopped nuts

Sift together dry ingredients. In a separate bowl, beat egg; stir in milk, honey, and melted butter. Stir in dry ingredients, stirring only enough to moisten flour. Spread into 8 by 8-inch lightly greased pan. Cover with honey topping (made by creaming butter and mixing in all other ingredients). Bake at 400 degrees for 20–30 minutes.

Source: From *Try These—Honey Recipes,* n.d., Illinois State Beekeepers Association.

All Honey Cake

½ C butter
1½ C honey
3 eggs
3 C flour

3 t baking powder
¾ t salt
¾ C milk

Cream butter and honey until light and fluffy; beat in eggs 1 at a time. Sift together dry ingredients and add to creamed mixture, alternating with milk. Pour batter into a 9 by 13-inch pan. Bake at 350 degrees for 45 minutes.

Source: Try These—Honey Recipes, n.d., Illinois State Beekeepers Association.

Banana Bundt Cake

This is my own recipe, developed in an effort to deal with bananas that inevitably turn brown before they're eaten.

⅔ C butter
1 C sugar
⅓ C honey
3 eggs
1 T lemon juice
3 medium bananas, mashed

2 C flour
⅔ t allspice
1⅓ t baking powder
1 t baking soda
⅓ C water
1 C chopped nuts (optional)

Cream together butter, sugar, and honey. Beat in eggs and lemon juice. Add mashed bananas. Sift together flour, allspice, baking powder, and baking soda. Add flour and water to creamed mixture alternately, beginning and ending with flour. Nuts can be folded in at this point. Grease and flour a Bundt pan and pour in batter. Bake at 350 degrees for 50–55 minutes, or until a toothpick inserted into cake comes out clean. Cool in pan 10–15 minutes; continue cooling on wire rack. Top with confectioner's sugar or lemon or vanilla glaze.

Bienenstich (Bee-Sting Cake)

Martin Hauser, a former graduate student in entomology at the University of Illinois at Urbana-Champaign, provided this recipe and related its history. "As usual," he explained, "there are conflicting theories about the bienenstich. The first one is that it is made without honey, the second one is that there is honey involved. . . . The name has at least 2 theories. One is that the sweet, creamy filling attracts bees, and people were stung when they ate the cake outdoors; the second theory is that two German towns were rivals, Linz am Rhein and Andernach. . . . One morning, men from the one town tried to attack 2 boys seeking honey from local beehives. When they saw the men approach, the boys threw the hives at them, and the attackers ran home. To celebrate their victory the boys created a new kind of cake and named it bienenstich."

Dough

2 C flour	pinch of salt
1½ t instant yeast	2 T sugar
¼ C milk	1 egg
1 t sugar	¼ C butter

Almond-Pudding Mix

1 pkg. (3 oz.) vanilla pudding	¼ C sugar
¼ C sugar	1½ C sliced almonds
2 C milk	¼ C butter
½ C whipping (or double) cream	1 C whipping (or double) cream
3½ T honey	

To make the dough: Build a little volcano with the flour. Warm the milk, and mix in the yeast. Add the teaspoon of sugar to the milk and pour into the center of the flour. Then gently mix the dough and let it rise for 15 minutes in a warm place. Then add salt, 2 T sugar, egg, and softened butter. Mix thoroughly. Place the dough in a plastic container, close, and place in warm water. When the lid pops open after 20 minutes the yeast dough is ready.

Place the dough on a floured surface and flatten it into a rectangle before placing it onto a paper-lined baking sheet and letting it stand another 20 minutes.

To make the almond-pudding mix: Combine the vanilla pudding powder with 3 T sugar and ¼ C milk. Heat the rest of the milk and whisk the vanilla pudding mix into it until creamy. Set aside. In a saucepan, add ½ C cream to 3½ T honey and ¼ C sugar; heat until bubbling. Remove from stove and stir in almonds. Place the almond mixture on top of the dough. Bake at 400 degrees for 15 minutes, until the almonds are golden. Let the cake cool, then slit its sides with a long knife and separate the almond topping from the dough.

To assemble, mix 3 T warm butter with the reserved vanilla pudding, Whip 1 C cream and combine with pudding. Place the pudding–whipped cream mix on top of the dough. Then place the almond layer on top of the pudding–whipped cream layer. Refrigerate for a short time before serving.

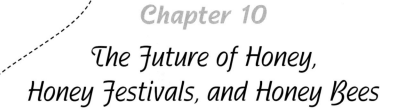

Chapter 10

The Future of Honey,
Honey Festivals, and Honey Bees

*E*very year, the town of Black Mountain, N.C., holds a sourwood honey festival. Sourwood (*Oxydendrum arboretum*) is a plant restricted to the southeastern United States (and abundant only in north Georgia and western North Carolina), and the light amber, aromatic honey made from its nectar is famous for its spicy taste and fine quality. But the thirty-second festival, in August 2009, was something of a disappointment. There was no sourwood honey to be had. Why the honey crop failed to materialize was an open question; some blamed spring rains or a drought the previous year. There was also the lingering fear that the North Carolina bees might have been struck by yet another mysterious ailment of the sort that seems to afflict honey bees at regular intervals.

North Carolina is far from alone. Honey production is experiencing wild fluctuations around the world. At the September 2009 meeting of the International Federation of Beekeepers Associations, Apimondia, attendees were given an update on the world honey situation. Overall, global production was estimated at 1.3 million metric tons, with the largest amount, 37 percent, coming from Asia. Honey production in the United States decreased from a hundred thousand metric tons (220,000,000 pounds) in 2000 to seventy-three thousand (161,000,000 pounds) in 2008. In Canada, the 2008 honey crop was down 35 percent from the previous year. Honey production in parts of Europe declined by almost 50 percent as well. Estimates for 2009 around the globe were less than optimistic.

Although there are many possible explanations for the decline in honey production (e.g., drought, antidumping laws, and conversion of cropland to biofuel feedstock production), one major explanation is that the number of honey bees has declined. In the fall of 2006, a mysterious phenomenon first materialized whereby the oldest bees in a colony, the foragers who leave the hive to collect nectar and pollen, vanish without a trace, leaving behind the queen with a few young nurses and larvae. Without foragers, a hive cannot replenish its food supply and effectively collapses. This phenomenon, ultimately called colony collapse disorder (CCD), was particularly disturbing because there were no dead bodies to account for the missing foragers. They just seemed to vanish. Although there had been intermittent disappearances in the past, none had ever been as widespread and long-lasting. Ultimately, thirty-five states were affected, and CCD brought about a 40 percent reduction in the number of honey bees. Estimates for 2009—seventy-five thousand metric tons (165 million pounds)—were on a par with the smallest honey crop since the USDA began keeping track of production in 1947. The phenomenon may be abating. Surveys conducted by the Apiary Inspectors of America pegged CCD losses in America's managed honey bee colonies during the winter of 2009 at 29 percent, a decline from estimates of 36 and 32 percent in the winters of 2006–2007 and 2007–2008, respectively. But annual losses of more than a quarter of America's bees are not sustainable.

Honey bees are beset by a staggering diversity of problems. The accidental introduction in the 1980s of two parasitic mites, the tracheal mite and the varroa mite, led to sharp decreases in the number of bees; between 1947 and 2005, colony numbers in the United States declined more than 40 percent, from 5.9 million to 2.4 million. These losses were exacerbated by the escalating demand for pollination services for fruit, nut, and vegetable crops, particularly almonds. Adding insult to injury, the varroa mite is a vector, or carrier, of at least five different viral diseases against which bees have apparently few defenses. The pesticides used to control the mites inside the hive are taking a toll on bees, as are the agricultural chemicals the bees inevitably encounter as they forage across an increasingly toxic agricultural landscape.

Although the honey bee is native to Europe, honey is as American as apple pie; in fact, without honey bees America may never have had apple pies. Honey bees accompanied some of the earliest colonists; William Blackstone, the first inhabitant of what would become the city of Boston, brought them from Europe to pollinate his apple trees in Massachusetts. Four hundred years later, we could manage as a nation without honey—we eat on average less than 1½ pounds per person annually, compared with a whopping 156 pounds of sugar and high-fructose corn syrup per person—but we can't manage without the honey bee.

Honey has so much to offer beyond sweetness. Eating honey helps keep honey bees in business, and busy honey bees help sustain natural and agricultural ecosystems around the world. Honey desserts are ecologically guilt-free, so enjoy them at every opportunity.

What Others Have Said about Honey

"For the rest, whatever we have got has been by infinite labor, and search, and ranging through every corner of nature; the difference is that instead of dirt and poison, we have rather chosen to fill our hives with honey and wax, thus furnishing making with the two noblest of things, which are sweetness and light" (Jonathan Swift, Irish author, 1667–1745).

"Nothing but money is sweeter than honey" (Benjamin Franklin, author, politician, and scientist, 1705–90).

"If you go in search of honey, you must expect to be stung by bees" (Joseph Joubert, French essayist, 1754–1824).

"If you want to gather honey, don't kick over the beehive" (Dale Carnegie, American writer and entrepreneur, 1888–1955).

"'Well,' said Pooh, 'what I like best——' and then he had to stop and think. Because although Eating Honey was a very good thing to do, there was a moment just before you began to eat it which was better than when you were, but he didn't know what it was called" (A. A. Milne, 1882–1956).

Honey Festivals

Al Seef Honey Festival (January in Sri Lanka)
Dubai Honey Festival (February)
Beeline Festival (April in Cambridge Mass.)
Tupelo Honey Festival (May in Wewahitchka, Fla.)
New York City Honey Festival (June)
Locana Honey Festival (July in Borgata Pratolungo, Italy)
Firestone Honey Festival (August in Firestone, Colo.)
Kleefeld Honey Festival (August in Kleefeld, Manitoba, Canada)
Dagangshan Long Yan Honey Festival (August in Taiwan)
Breathitt County Honey Festival (September in Jackson, Ky.)
Clarkson Honeyfest (September in Clarkson, Ky.)

Lithopolis Honeyfest (September in Lithopolis, Ohio)

West Virginia Honey Festival (September in Parkersburg)

Nikiti Honey Festival (October in Nikiti, Greece)

Châtillon Honey Festival, Italy (October in the Aosta Valley's honey capital)

Warialda Honey Festival (November in Warialda, NSW, Australia)

Minco Honey Festival (December in Minco, Okla., home of the "largest honey processing facility in the state")

References

Allsop, K. A., and J. B. Miller. 1996. "Honey Revisited: A Reappraisal of Honey in Preindustrial Diets." *British Journal of Nutrition* 75:513–20.

Barrett, J. 1981. *Cooking with Honey.* North Adams, Mass.: Storey Publishing.

"Bee Raw" at www.worldpantry.com/cgi-bin/ncommerce3/ExecMacro/beeraw/servents.d2w/report (accessed March 8, 2010).

Berto, H. 1972. *Cooking with Honey.* New York: Gramercy Publishing.

Bogdanov, S., T. Jurendic, R. Sieber, and P. Gallmann. 2008. "Honey for Nutrition and Health: A Review." *Journal of the American College of Nutrition* 27:677–89.

California Honey Advisory Board. 1970. *Gems of Gold with Honey.* Sonoma: California Honey Advisory Board.

Crane, E., ed. 1975. *Honey: A Comprehensive Survey.* London: Heinemann.

———. 1999. *The World History of Beekeeping and Honey Hunting.* London: Gerald Duckworth.

Distretto Turistico dei Laghi e Valli d'Ossola at www. distrettolaghi.eu/en/index .php?option=com_content&task=view&id=26&Itemid=41 (accessed March 8, 2010).

Frankel, S., G. Robinson, and M. R. Berenbaum. 1998. "Antioxidant Capacity and Correlated Characteristics of Fourteen Monofloral Honeys." *Journal of Apicultural Research* 37:27–31.

Glyngell, S. 2007. *The Independent,* April 29.

Lonik, L. 1981. *The Healthy Taste of Honey: Bee People's Recipes, Anecdotes and Lore.* Virginia Beach, Va.: Donning.

Mckibben, J., and N. J. Engeseth. 2002. "Honey as a Protective Agent against Lipid Oxidation in Muscle Foods." *Journal of Agricultural Food Chemistry* 50:592–95.

Molan, P. C. 1992. "The Antibacterial Activity of Honey, 1: The Nature of the Antibacterial Activity." *Bee World* 73: 5–28.

Niall, M. 2003. *Covered in Honey: The Amazing Flavors of Varietal Honey.* Emmaus, Pa.: Rodale Press.

Perlman, D. 1971. *The Magic of Honey: Cooking with Honey.* New York: Galahad Books.

Phillips, K., M. Carlsen, and R. Blomhoff. 2009. "Total Antioxidant Content of Alternatives to Refined Sugar." *Journal of the American Dietetic Association* 109:64–71.

Popescu, C. 1997. *The Honey Cookbook.* Upavon, Wilts., U.K.: Cavalier Cookbooks.

Schneider, A. 2008. "Honey Laundering." *Seattle Post Intelligencer,* Dec. 30.

Vegan Society. 2010. "Memorandum of Association of the Vegan Society" at www.veganso-ciety.com/uploadedFiles/AboutUs/Articles-of-Association-Nov-09.pdf (accessed March 8, 2010).

"Why Is Honey Kosher?" at www.jewishcooking.org/kosherfood/honey.html (accessed March 7, 2010).

Wilson, B. 2004. *The Hive: The Story of the Honey Bee and Us.* New York: Thomas Dunne Books.

Index

Flan de miel (Honey Flan), 111
flesh-eating bacterium (MRSA), 13
flowers, 6–7
Franklin, Benjamin, 149
French Gingerbread, 84
French Honey Loaf, 133–34
fried desserts. *See* no-bake, boiled, and fried
    desserts
frostings and glazes
    for Apricot Bars, 45
    for Beehive Bread, 86
    for Glazed Greek Crescent Cookies, 29
    for Honey Fudge Cake, 131
    for Honey-Glazed Bran muffins, 79
    for Lebkuchen (Honey Spice Cake), 56,
        57, 58
    for Mostaccioli Cookies, 68–69
    for Pão de mel (Brazilian Honey-Spice
        Bread), 84–85
    for Pfefferkuchen, 59–60
    for Pfeffernüsse, 27
    for Quick Coffee Cake, 140
    for South African Honey Lemon Biscuits,
        35
    for Spiced Honey Cakes (Leckerli), 56
    for Swiss Leckerli, 41
    for Yoyo Biscuits, 34
fructose, 7, 19
Fudge Cake, Honey, 131

G
Gatnabour (Armenian Rice Pudding), 110
Gemara, 11–12
Georgics (Vergil), 5
gingerbread
    First-Prize Honey, 83
    French, 84
gingersnaps
    Honey, 54
    No-Bake Orange Ginger Cookie Balls, 91

Glazed Greek Crescent Cookies, 29
glazes. *See* frostings and glazes
glucose, 7, 19
Glyngell, Skye, 20–21
goat milk
    Honey and Curd (Mel i mató), 114
Gourmet Magazine, 21
Gram Bea's Saskatoon Pie, 114–15
Grandma Berenbaum's Challah, 77
Grandma Jesse's Imberlach, 91
Greek Doughnuts (Loukoumades), 101–2
Greek Nut Cake (Adrienne's Karidopeta), 136
Greek Ricotta and Honey Pie (Melopita), 117
Greeks, ancient, 4

H
Hamentaschen, 62
Hangop with Blackberries, Honey, and Mint,
    112–13
Haystacks, Honey, 31
Hazelnut Teiglach, 66
hazelnuts
    Aachener Nussprinten, 53
    Beehives, 46
    Grandma Jesse's Imberlach, 91
    Mostaccioli Cookies, 68–69
    Teiglach, 66
Hermits, First-Prize Honey, 25
hive design, 5–6
Homer, 4–5
honey: about, 3–4; adulterated, 22; in ancient
    times, 4–5; classifying, 11–12; in colonial
    times, 5; color and scent, 8, 14; crystal-
    lized, 19; decline in production, 147;
    health benefits, 13–15; how bees make
    it, 6–9; liquid, 19–20; vs. sugar, 10–11, 13,
    15, 19; toxins, 8–9; types, 20–22; vitamins
    and minerals, 8, 13–14; why bees eat it, 9
Honey: A Comprehensive Survey (Crane), 15
honey festivals, 147, 149–50

May Berenbaum is Swanlund Professor of Entomology at the University of Illinois at Urbana-Champaign. She is a Fellow of the American Academy of Arts and a member of the National Academy of Sciences. Her other books include *Ninety-Nine Gnats, Nits, and Nibblers*; *Ninety-Nine More Maggots, Mites, and Munchers*; *Bugs in the System: Insects and Their Impact on Human Affairs*; *Buzzwords: A Scientist Muses on Sex, Bugs, and Rock 'n' Roll*; and *The Earwig's Tail: A Modern Bestiary of Multi-legged Legends.*

The University of Illinois Press
is a founding member of the
Association of American University Presses.

Designed by Kelly Gray
Composed in 9.5/14 Helvetica Neue
with Agfa Nadianne display
by Jim Proefrock
at the University of Illinois Press
Manufactured by Bang Printing

University of Illinois Press
1325 South Oak Street
Champaign, IL 61820-6903
www.press.uillinois.edu